KV-013-708

4/7/71 45245 0302

WITHDRAWN
FROM
LEARNING RESOURCE
CENTRE
KINGSTON COLLEGE

KINGSTON COLLEGE

00175883

STUDYING BIRDS IN THE GARDEN

Other books by Terry Jennings:

Mysteries of Animal Behaviour
Wild Life in the Garden
Animals in the Home and Classroom
A Background to Biochemistry
Collecting from Nature

Studying Birds in the Garden

by **Terry Jennings**, B.Sc
*Lecturer in Biology at Keswick Hall
College of Education*

Illustrated by Michael Strand

WHEATON
A Member of the Pergamon Group

Pergamon Press Ltd, Headington Hill Hall,
Oxford OX3 OBW
Pergamon Press Inc., Maxwell House,
Fairview Park, Elmsford, New York 10523
Pergamon of Canada Ltd,
PO Box 9600, Don Mills,
Ontario, M3C 2T9
Pergamon Press (Aust.) Pty Ltd,
19a Boundary Street, Rushcutters Bay,
N.S.W. 2011, Australia

Acc. No. 00175883
Class No. 598.2
Date Rec 18.9.75
Order No F13864

Copyright © Terry Jennings 1975

All rights reserved. No part of this
publication may be reproduced, stored in a
retrieval system, or transmittted, in any
form or by any means, electronic,
mechanical, photocopying, recording or
otherwise, without the prior permission of
Pergamon Press Ltd.

First edition 1975

Printed and bound in Great Britain by
A. Wheaton & Co., Exeter

ISBN 0 08 017802 2

Contents

Introduction

Bird-watching has two great advantages as a hobby. It is an open-air pursuit that you can carry on throughout the year, anywhere from the middle of a large city to the wildest moorlands and mountains. And it needs no expensive equipment to start with, though you will certainly want a pair of binoculars when you have progressed a little way.

This book aims to tell you some of the many ways in which you can learn about wild birds without moving far from home. The first chapter discusses general techniques of bird-watching that apply everywhere, but later chapters describe simple observations, experiments, projects and other activities that you can carry out in a garden, park, square or playing field.

Do not be deterred if you have only a small garden, or even none at all. I have lived in my present home for three years, and during that time, in a back garden which measures about 12 m by 12 m, I have recorded 46 species of birds actually in the garden and many more passing over. Those alighting in the garden included some unexpected ones such as a pheasant and a moorhen, and several less common species including a cirl bunting, a brambling, a flock of long-tailed tits, and several goldcrests. Any small public garden, park or piece of waste ground will have its own particular list of bird species that you can study.

There are already many books describing the art of bird-watching. Where I hope mine is different is that it attempts to take the young bird-watcher beyond the stage of looking for 'new' birds and measuring the success of his activities by the number of rare birds seen, to the even more interesting and rewarding task of finding out more about the habits and behaviour of birds and trying to interpret these actions. This is the way to become an ornithologist rather than a mere bird-spotter.

CHAPTER ONE

Starting Bird-watching

OBSERVATION AND IDENTIFICATION

You will not be able to progress very far in your study of birds until you are able to identify accurately the common local birds and some of the less common species that you see. With birds as with people, finding out names is the first step towards getting to know them better.

Closely linked with identification is observation, since identification depends to a great extent on the ability to observe correctly. No one can teach you how to observe, but it is quite possible for you to develop your own powers of observation so that, as time goes by, your sight becomes keener and your other senses become more alert.

There is no easy path to becoming an expert bird-watcher; no short cut that avoids the expenditure of much time and patience. No one expects to become a good cricketer or pianist without much practice, and the same applies to bird-watching. You will soon find that the more birds you watch, the easier it becomes to identify them, as you get to know the points to look for.

The one essential piece of equipment, apart from a notebook and pencil, is a good field guide book to birds, showing each species in colour (see page 115). The best ones point out some special feature or features in the bird's structure or colouring by which it can be easily identified.

But first, before you use your bird book, you might like to try this little exercise to improve your powers of observation. Go out for a walk taking with you a notebook and pencil. When you come across the first common bird that you can identify, stop and have a good look at it. When it has gone, make a note of as many of the bird's features as you can. Later, at home, take out your bird book and compare your notes with the picture and description given in the book. How many important features did you miss? Would you have been able to identify the bird from your notes alone if it had been a species with which you were not familiar?

Repeat this exercise several times with birds that you are able to identify positively, and then try making notes of the important details of a species that you are not able to identify on sight. A park is a good place to start, particularly if it has a lake or pond with waterfowl, since the birds will be tamer and easier to approach.

You must train yourself to notice as much as you can in a very short time—for often you may have the bird in full view only for a few seconds—and then write down the details about it as soon as possible afterwards.

Try to make your notes under certain general headings. You may not be able to fill in something under each heading every time, but anything you can note down will help.

Here are some of the things you might consider:

1 Size of bird

As you will know how large a sparrow is compared with, say a town pigeon, you can easily decide whether the unidentified bird is larger or smaller. We might say that a blackbird is half way between the two or that a swan is much larger than either.

Fig. 1. Comparing the size of birds. From left to right: house sparrow, town pigeon, swan

2 Shape

Get to know the shapes of birds. A few birds are round and small, as is for example the common wren. Sparrow-sized and stout-looking birds include the robin and greenfinch. The wagtails and buntings are also sparrow-sized but slender and elegant. Ducks are generally large and plump, and have short tails and long necks. The shape of the tail and wings is also sometimes a useful guide. As the bird flies away, note if its tail and wings are long, short, pointed or rounded.

Fig. 2. The shape of birds. From left to right: wren, robin, greenfinch, wagtail, duck

3 General colour

This is an all-important feature. A small black and white bird which runs rapidly over the ground and bobs its tail is easily recognized as a pied wagtail. A much larger bird with burnished white and black plumage is a magpie. A round all-brown bird, very small with a cocked-up tail, is the common wren.

These are the more obvious features, but not all birds have such conspicuous colouring. You should, in this case, note the bird's main colour, and also any conspicuous marks, patches and stripes, with their position on the bird as far as you can judge. Bars and patches on the wings and at the base of the tail are always important points to look for. If you wish to learn the correct names for the various parts of the bird's body to help you with your descriptions, Fig. 3 will be useful.

4 Beak, feet and legs

The colour and shape of these are very important points to note.

From the shape of a bird's beak one can learn something of its feeding habits (Fig. 4). Slender, short and pointed beaks generally belong to the insect-eating warblers. The seed-eating finches, sparrows and buntings have conical, short and powerful beaks, whilst birds such as the rook, starling and jackdaw, which probe into the soil for worms and grubs have dagger-like beaks. The beaks of the great number of wading birds which search deep into mud, sand and soft wet ground for animal food are even longer and more slender, and those of the curlew, whimbrel and avocet for some strange reason are curved. Thrushes

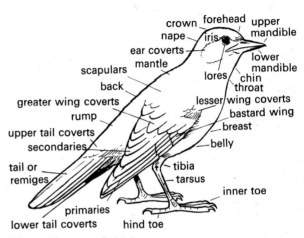

Fig. 3. The parts of a bird

and blackbirds come into two feeding groups since they will eat fruit, berries and seeds as well as worms, snails and insects. To cope with this varied diet, their beaks are short, strong and pointed. Ducks, geese and swans have shallow, spoon-shaped beaks that are used when searching for vegetable and animal matter in the water.

Owls, hawks and other birds of prey have modified beaks and feet for catching and dealing with their victims. Their beaks are strong and hooked for tearing the food apart, whilst they have feet with long, curved, needle-sharp talons for gripping and piercing their victims when they are first caught.

Most birds have three toes which point forward, with a small toe which points backwards, and sharp claws (Fig. 5). These are the so-called *passerine* or perching birds. In perching birds which have taken to living much on the ground, such as the larks, the hind claw has lost its curve and is long and straight. Another group of ground-living birds such as the partridge, grouse and some other game birds, have a hind toe with its tiny claw so small and situated so high up on the back of the foot that it is almost useless. This is also true of many water birds, including the gulls, and in some sea birds such as razorbills and guillemots, the hind toe has disappeared altogether.

Some birds which climb trees, notably woodpeckers, have two claws directed forward and two backwards. Other climbers like the tree creeper and nuthatch are provided with one extra strong hind toe and claw to help support the grip of the three forward toes. Owls and cuckoos can apparently switch from three toes in front and one behind, to two each as the need arises!

Ducks, geese, swans, gulls and cormorants have webbed feet; so have terns, skuas, guillemots, razorbills and puffins. But not all swimming birds have webs. The moorhen is an excellent swimmer but its long slender toes are useful for walking over floating vegetation. The coot has neither one thing nor the other, its toes are lobed. Grebes, divers and a few wading birds also have either toe lobes or in some cases partially webbed feet.

Fig. 4. Some bills and beaks

In addition, a few birds—heron, nightjar, cormorant and gannet—have a curious 'toothed' edge to the central claw, which is used for preening.

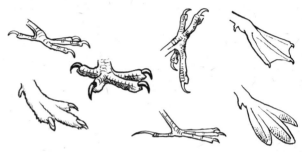

Fig. 5. Birds' feet

5 Gait and flight

Was the unknown bird on the ground, perching or flying? If it was on the ground and moving, did it hop, walk or run? Hopping birds include the sparrow, robin and chaffinch, and many others, while starlings and the various species of wagtail are among the small birds that walk or run according to their mood.

In trying to identify birds in flight it is possible to eliminate some and recognize others simply by the way they fly, and of course by their size.

Some birds such as the starling, wren and kingfisher fly in a straight line with rapidly whirring wings. Others, including the partridge and pheasant, fly straight but glide at intervals with wings outstretched. Certain other species partly fold their wings for brief intervals, causing them to fly with a curious up-and-down *undulating* motion. These include woodpeckers, the jay and the little owl.

The largest British birds, such as the heron and the swan, flap their wings slowly as they fly in a

Fig. 6. Flight of starling and woodpecker

straight line, as if flying were hard work—as indeed it often is in bad weather. On the other hand, certain birds seem to enjoy flying and spend much time in fine weather gliding and soaring in the sky, and being pushed upwards by warm air currents like glider pilots. The kestrel is skilled at hovering for quite a long time in the same place. Many other birds, particularly the birds of prey, have this ability to stop in mid-air and hover, however briefly. The king-fisher will hover over water when searching for the small fish it lives on, but the real expert in this field is the magnificent osprey. For hunters, swifts, swallows and martins are quite noisy in flight, but their narrow crescent-shaped wings easily enable them to out-fly and out-manoeuvre the flying insects on which they feed.

6 Call-notes and song

Any sound you may hear the bird make is an especially important clue to its identity. Unfortunately it is by no means easy to describe bird song in words. Sparrows have a language of 'cheeps' and 'chissicks',

which you will hear if you listen to their conversation. The blackbird makes its familiar loud rattling alarm call when it is disturbed by man, a cat or a hawk. The yellow-hammer or yellow bunting has one of the songs most often described in books, usually as 'a-little-bit-of-bread-and-no-cheese!'. One of the most confusing bird songs is that of the starling. This species is a wonderful mimic and you may hear it reproduce the songs and call-notes of many other birds, as well as various clanking and mechanical noises and even, on occasion, 'wolf whistles'. So beware of saying that you heard a curlew or a night-ingale if you are anywhere near Trafalgar Square or some other large starling roost at sunset!

It takes time and experience to recognise bird songs but if you have a good sense of rhythm and an ear for music, it is not a difficult skill to acquire. A good set of bird-song gramophone records will help no end, and if you have a tape-recorder you might like to build up a collection of bird songs of your own. How to do this is described on pages 101-103.

Write down as many of these details as possible, while the bird is still in sight if you can. After the bird has gone you can add the essential background information such as the date and time, place, type of country, what birds if any were accompanying it, and the weather conditions, particularly if there is any possibility of the bird having been a visitor from overseas.

The place, and type of country (heath, oak-wood, lake, pond, etc.) are very important since each bird has its natural home or habitat. Of the water birds, for example, gannets, razorbills, shearwaters, petrels, puffins and eider ducks are found only on salt water. Amongst land birds, goldcrests, tits, tawny owls, jays and many warblers are never seen in open, tree-less country unless they happen to be migrating. On the other hand, starlings, wheatears, rooks, lapwings, and short-eared owls almost always feed out in the open, although starlings and rooks return to trees to roost.

Another reason why the place where you saw the bird should be carefully recorded is that not all species are uniformly distributed throughout the country. The carrion-crow, for instance, is a resident throughout England, Wales and southern Scotland, and in spite of its unpopularity is, in places, common. In the Highlands of Scotland, Ireland and the Isle of Man, another species, the hooded crow, replaces it. Similarly, in England and Wales the nuthatch and marsh tit are familiar birds of woodland and gardens, but in most parts of Scotland they are rare.

Here is a specimen note along the lines just described:

Size: Slightly smaller than a sparrow.

Shape: Fairly streamlined.

General colour: Back streaked and mottled with brown. Undersides whitish. Wings barred with pale brown.

Bill and legs: Bill brown, slender and curved down-wards. Legs brown and the feet quite large for such a small bird.

Gait and flight: At first thought to be a mouse as it ran up the trunk of an oak tree. Movements rapid but jerky—frequently made sideways jumps. Seemed to be using tail like a shooting-stick to support body.

Call-notes: High-pitched 'cheep cheep'.

Habitat: Oak tree, Kensington Gardens.

Weather: Cold and frosty but sunny. Slight breeze from N.E.

Date and place: London, 1st January, 1975.

The next step in the identification process is to look through your bird book, first at the pictures and then the descriptions, to see which species fits all the details in your notes. The small size of the bird in the notes written above immediately rules out many species, and there are not many small birds with such drab coloration. Perhaps the most unusual feature of all is the slender curved bill. These details do in fact identify the bird as a tree-creeper which is the only small brown bird that climbs trees in a mouse-like way.

Do not be discouraged if at first you do not succeed in spotting the all-important feature before the bird disappears. Keep looking, try to get closer next time, and eventually, after much practice, you will have no problems with identification.

GETTING CLOSER TO BIRDS

Approaching birds closely calls for some degree of skill and cunning and also a knowledge of their senses. The sense of smell in birds is poor, but their sight and hearing are extremely keen. Although a bird's ear is completely hidden under feathers, it is more sensitive than ours for we cannot hear worms moving underground or grubs boring deep inside a piece of rotting timber, as some birds can.

In many cases it is better to remain still and quiet and wait for the birds to come close to you. The small birds that feed in hedgerows, generally work their way along the hedge, and if you hide yourself against the hedge some distance in front of them they will probably come very close to you.

This technique is not always successful though, and if the birds will not come towards you, you must go nearer to them. Fortunately we can make use of one of the few defects in a bird's eyesight. Many small birds seem to have difficulty in recognizing large objects when they are very close to them. To a small bird a human is a large object and if you remain perfectly still the bird will not notice you. As soon as you move, you become visible immediately to the birds and alarm them. When approaching a bird you must use whatever cover is available. Try to keep a hedge, bank, wall, tree trunk, bush or boulder between yourself and your quarry. If you are not able to walk behind these objects, keep in front of them so that the bird does not see you outlined against the sky.

As far as possible, wear quiet clothing for bird-watching, olive-green, khaki or light brown, rather than white or bright red or blue, in order to merge as much as possible with the background. The type of waterproof wear that rustles every time you move should be avoided.

If you have to cross open ground to get a better view of a bird, do it very slowly and, if you can, do a 'Red Indian crawl'. If you are walking over the type of ground where you cannot move quietly, perhaps where there is a thick carpet of dead leaves, it is a help to approach the bird from down-wind, that is with

Fig. 7. How to make yourself invisible

Fig. 8. The right and the wrong way to use a tree when bird-watching.

the wind blowing in your face, so that any noise you make is not carried to the bird. It is also best to keep the sun behind you, so that the birds are in sunlight and clearly visible, whilst you are in shadow. This can have disadvantages if you are likely to be silhouetted against a bright sky.

Fig. 9. How to cross open ground to get closer to a bird (and how not to do it)

Even without binoculars, the skilled bird-watcher can usually get a good view of any bird because he is able to guess what it is going to do next, and can use this knowledge to get within a few metres of it.

MAKING A HIDE

One advantage of studying birds in a garden is that you already have a comfortable hide from which to watch: your house. If your garden is large, or if you wish to study birds in the country or even on a piece of waste ground or a playing field, you will sooner or later need a hide. It is surprising how many

birds—and other creatures, you will see at close quarters merely by hiding from them, and exercising patience.

A simple hide is not difficult or expensive to make. Four pieces of broom handle are needed, each about 160 cm long, with one end of each sharpened to a point so that it can easily be pushed or driven into the ground. If you wish to make the task of carrying the hide easier, you can cut each post in half and fit a short length of metal tubing onto each of the four lower sections of the poles, into which the four upper sections will fit (Fig. 10a). Insert two screw eyes, about 2 cm apart, near the top of each of the four posts (Fig. 10b).

The ideal material for making the hide is waterproof tent canvas, but this can be expensive and is not always easy to obtain. A fairly good substitute is hessian lined with another material such as old sheeting or curtaining which will make it opaque, so that the birds will not be able to see you moving about inside. The material you use should be at least 90 cm wide. Whatever width is chosen will affect the width of the hide, and the four pieces of stout wire that join the four posts together (Fig. 10b) will have to be cut accordingly.

The material should be cut in two lengths, each about 450 cm long, and laid in the form of a cross (Fig. 10c). If the material used is not waterproof, a square of plastic or stout polythene sheeting may be laid where the two strips cross each other. This waterproof layer can then be stitched together (Fig. 10c). The fourth pair of sides are pinned together with safety pins when you are inside the hide.

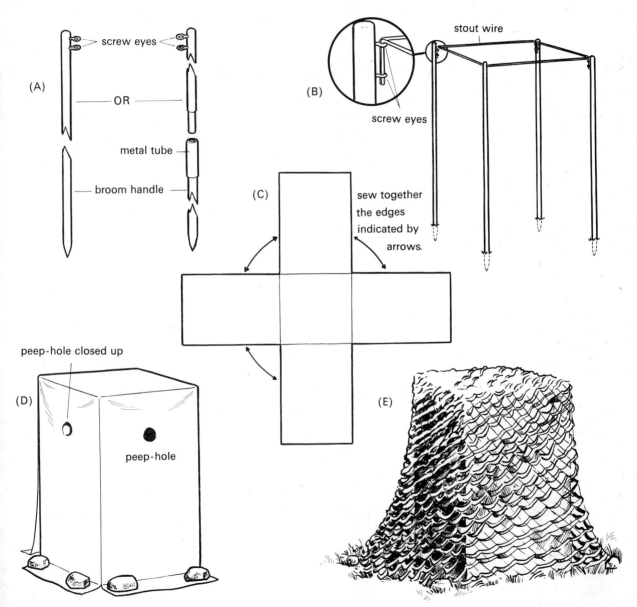

(A)

screw eyes

OR

metal tube

broom handle

(B)

stout wire

screw eyes

(C)

sew together
the edges
indicated by
arrows.

peep-hole closed up

(D)

peep-hole

(E)

Fig. 10. Making a hide

Cut a peep-hole flap in each of the four sides (Fig. 10d), but keep covered, by means of a safety pin or button, those peep-holes not actually in use.

In windy weather you may have to anchor the bottom of the hide with bricks, large stones or pieces of wood to prevent them from flapping, and scaring the birds.

As far as the birds are concerned there is no need to camouflage the hide, but it may be necessary in areas where human intruders are likely to be a nuisance. The method of camouflage used by the army of covering the object to be hidden with a strip of wide-mesh netting through which strips of brown, green or some other appropriately coloured cloth has been woven, is most effective.

When going to the hide it is always best to be accompanied by a friend who then departs, because birds seem to be unable to count, and will associate his departure with the removal of human danger. A small folding stool or wooden box will enable you to pass the time in comfort, and a small pocket torch is essential to enable you to see your notebook or sketch-pad.

From your hide you will be able to see many intimate details of bird behaviour; however a word of warning is necessary here: used properly, by skilled ornithologists, a hide presents an excellent means of studying the nesting behaviour of birds. But it is all too easy for the keen young bird-watcher to disturb the nesting birds and so cause them to desert their eggs or young, or for his hide to draw the attention of cats, grey squirrels, egg-collectors and other pests to the nest. I would therefore strongly advise you not to use a hide near a nest until you have had a great deal of experience in the use of hides under a wide range of other conditions. If however, a bird should build its nest near to a window of your house or garden shed, then you have an excellent ready-made hide which, if used carefully, will cause no distress to the birds.

One final reminder: when you are using a hide on someone else's land, do make sure that you have permission first.

BUYING AND USING BINOCULARS

Once you are really set on becoming a bird-watcher, it will not be long before you want to beg, borrow or buy a pair of binoculars or field glasses—the two names mean the same thing. Bird-watching requires little basic equipment, but a pair of binoculars is the one thing that most bird-watchers consider essential. They are expensive but they are well worth saving for, since they will make all the difference to your enjoyment of your hobby, and if looked after will last a lifetime.

When choosing binoculars, remember the main reason for using them is to reduce the apparent distance of the bird, so that it seems larger and nearer. However, there is a limit to the amount the binoculars will magnify if they are still to be useful for bird study. The more the binoculars magnify, the less clear is the image that can be seen through them and the narrower is the field of view. This often means that by the time you have successfully focused on the spot where you

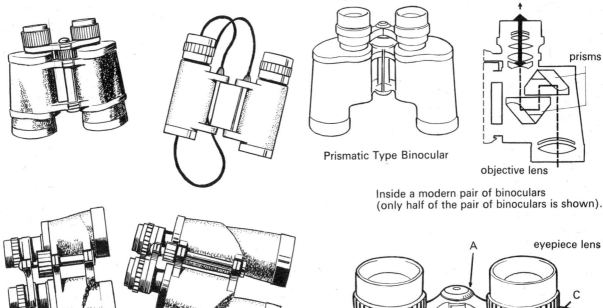

Prismatic Type Binocular

Inside a modern pair of binoculars
(only half of the pair of binoculars is shown).

Fig. 11. Some of the many kinds of binoculars

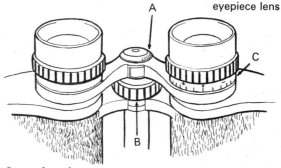

Centre focusing

A. Pupillary Scale
B. Centre Focusing Wheel
C. Dioptre Focusing Scale

last saw the bird it may have moved on, and the greatly enlarged background looks so different from the way it appeared to the naked eye when you first spotted the bird. Generally speaking, the higher the magnification, the more expensive the binoculars are, the heavier and bulkier they are to carry around, and the harder it is to hold them still.

The magnification should not be less than six times, better still seven, and best of all in my opinion is eight. Magnifications of nine and ten times are useful for long distance work, as on estuaries and cliffs, but not nearly so good for close-up work in gardens, parks and woods.

Focusing: The right eye should be closed or covered and the binocular should be set for the left eye by means of the centre wheel. The left eye should then be closed or covered and if the image with the right eye is not clear, the dioptre scale on the right eye piece should be turned slowly from plus to minus, stopping at the point where the image is clearly defined. Both eyes have now been balanced and future focusing is achieved by centre focusing wheel only.

Fig. 12. The parts of a pair of binoculars

Now, what do those numbers written on binoculars, such as 10 × 40, 7 × 50 or 6 × 30, really mean? The first number in each case is the magnification. A 10 × sign indicates that an object will appear ten times larger through the binoculars than when viewed with the naked eye from the same distance, or to put it another way, with a 10 × binocular you can expect to see a bird 200 m away looking as though it were only 20 m away (that is 200 divided by 10).

After the multiplication sign there appears another, larger number (usually between 20 and 60). This is simply the diameter in millimetres of the objective lens (the large lens furthest from the eye). Thus 7 × 50 binoculars magnify seven times and have an objective lens 50 mm across.

For bird-watchers the most important figure of all is the one that is not usually written on binoculars—the exit pupil. The exit pupil can be seen by holding the binoculars at arms' length up to the light. The bigger the exit pupil, the clearer will be the image seen by the eye when the binoculars are used.

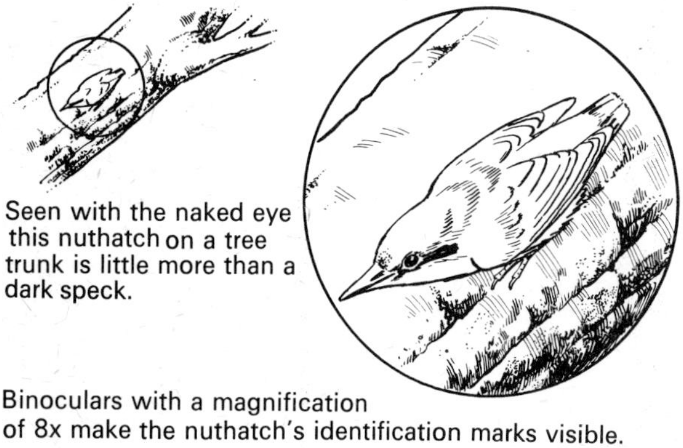

Seen with the naked eye this nuthatch on a tree trunk is little more than a dark speck.

Binoculars with a magnification of 8x make the nuthatch's identification marks visible.

Fig. 13. Why binoculars are very useful

We need not go into all the technical details here, but a measure of the size of the exit pupil can be obtained by dividing the diameter of the objective lens by the magnification. The result for 7 × 40 binoculars would be 5·7 mm (40 divided by 7) and for 8 × 30 it is 3·75 mm (30 divided by 8). Any value for the exit pupil over 3·75 mm is sufficient, and over 4 mm is even better.

Some manufacturers stamp on their binoculars a *field of view*. This is the width of the area you can see through the binoculars at a given distance. The field of view generally goes down as the magnification goes up.

Taking all the various factors into account, I would recommend a pair of 8 × 30 binoculars since they give sufficient magnification, a good clear image and wide field of view, without being too awkward and bulky to bring into action quickly or to use for long periods without strain.

If you go to a shop and ask to see only 8 × 30 binoculars, you will probably be shown a vast range of makes and prices. What you can afford will obviously be most important, but here are some other factors that should be borne in mind. The quality of the lenses and prisms that go to make up the binoculars is extremely important. Make sure that those you are considering are 'coated'. When you look at them (not through them), coated lenses should have a blue or yellow tinge. One word of warning, though: many binoculars are described as having coated lenses, but often only the front surface of the objective and eyepiece lenses are coated. These are useless, as there are at least ten glass surfaces in binoculars and all of them should be coated, for coating reduces the amount of reflection of light and gives a brighter, clearer image.

Another essential is that the binoculars should feel comfortable in your hands. You must be able to hold them quite still for a reasonable length of time and be able to focus them quickly. Make sure that your binoculars have a central focusing wheel, that is a centre screw which moves both eyepieces at the same time. If your right eye has a different focus from the left (as is the case with many people) there should also be a separate adjustment for one of the two eyepieces. When each lens has been set to suit your eyes, further focusing is made with the centre screw only. Speed is essential when a bird is flying towards you or away from you.

Hold the binoculars the wrong way round and look through them to make sure that there is no dirt on the eyepieces and also that the lenses have no scratches, chips, air-bubbles, or other flaws in them. Next check the working of the binoculars by holding them correctly and focusing on a fairly small distant object, such as a television aerial or flag-pole. If you bend the two halves of the binoculars so that your eyes fit easily into the eyepieces, and look through the centre of the lenses, you should, without straining your eyes, be able to see a bright single image which is not distorted in any way. It is equally important to check the close range to see how the binoculars can focus on nearer objects. You should be able to read a poster or the large print on a newspaper from a distance of about 6 m.

The fairly recent arrival on the market of quite

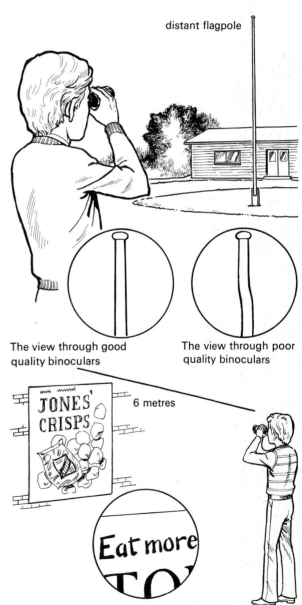

distant flagpole

The view through good quality binoculars

The view through poor quality binoculars

JONES' CRISPS

6 metres

Eat more TO

Fig. 14. Testing a pair of binoculars

inexpensive Japanese makes has brought binoculars within the reach of many more bird-watchers, but there are many different kinds to choose from, and the quality and performance varies greatly even in binoculars of the same make. You must test the binoculars yourself or obtain expert advice. Most reliable firms will allow you to take away binoculars against a deposit, so that you may test them and at least one firm dealing with postal as well as personal shoppers, will send them on fourteen days' free approval. If it is at all possible, before finally deciding which pair to buy, compare the quality of the image and the general workmanship of your binoculars, with those of a really good (and expensive) pair such as a Zeiss or a Swift Audubon.

When you use your binoculars, always start by hanging the lanyard (the strap attached to them) round your neck. Dropping them could mean an expensive repair bill or total loss. Be careful when you climb over hedges and stiles that the binoculars do not bang against your body, and never leave them about in the open, or anywhere, for long. When not in use these valuable pieces of equipment should be returned to their cases and kept in a dry clean place.

Practise using the binoculars frequently so that focusing becomes an automatic reaction. Clean the outside lenses regularly with a soft velvety piece of material, like the one used for cleaning spectacles. Never use a harsh scratchy cloth, or you may damage the lenses. The glass used in lenses looks hard but is in fact quite soft and easily scratched.

Finally, I would strongly advise you to ask your parents to take out an 'All Risks' insurance policy on your binoculars. This does not cost very much and frees you of some of the worries and fears of having the binoculars stolen or of seeing them tumble down a mountain-side or over a cliff.

KEEPING RECORDS

Once the art of identifying birds has been mastered, you may well ask: 'Where do I go from here?' Day after day you will be meeting the same bird species and, not unnaturally, you will want to make a scientific study of birds rather than merely looking for new species. This is where it is hoped that the projects and experiments given later on in this book will help you. However, it is convenient to mention here the great importance of careful and accurate note-taking.

If you have read the section dealing with identification you will no doubt have realised that it would be very difficult to keep all the information in your head, since it might be several hours before you are able to check your reference books and positively identify a species. A notebook is obviously essential.

Similarly, when you make scientific observations on birds, it is again essential to have your field notebook always with you and, so far as is possible, to write everything down within minutes if not seconds of seeing the bird. Memory is short, and can play some peculiar and annoying tricks after only an hour or two. The very act of writing notes is an aid to remembering what happened, as well as providing definite proof of what you saw.

Always write too much rather than too little, since unnecessary facts can always be left out later from your permanent record, whereas something you did not bother to record may later turn out to have been important. Every record should include the date, time and place, and any other information that might have any bearing on the bird's behaviour. In the case of records of migrating birds for instance, it would be very important to note the wind force and direction, the height and density of the clouds and, if possible, the air pressure as recorded by a barometer (the little book in **The Observer's** series, called **Weather** is a great help with this type of work). On the other hand, such details would not matter so much in a study of the feeding behaviour of young starlings.

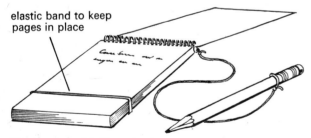

Fig. 15. A good field notebook

For making records in the field a stout notebook which easily fits the pocket is essential. It should have stiff covers to resist wear and prevent floppiness which makes writing or sketching awkward. A stout elastic band can be used to keep it closed and prevent the pages from becoming unnecessarily 'dog-eared'. Make your notes in pencil or waterproof ink so that dropping the book into a puddle will not wash away several weeks' or months' work.

As most of us are apt to scribble untidily when in the open air, often standing or sitting awkwardly, it is usually necessary to keep a permanent record of observations by neatly copying out the entries from the field notebook into another book. Your records could be in the form of a diary or entered under species headings, such as 'robin', 'blackbird', 'song thrush', and so on. In the latter case it is best to use a loose-leaf notebook so that you can add extra pages as the ones for the more common species become filled.

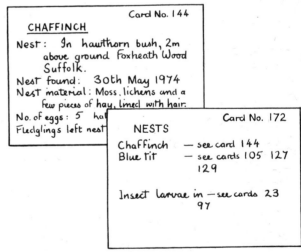

Fig. 16. A card index system for birds

A good index, including species, places, times of the year and different aspects of bird behaviour such as feeding, nest-building, courtship, fighting, preening, and so on, is a great help when you wish to consult past records. You might use a card index system for all your notes, and this will make it much easier to look up any individual subject. Enter the bird's name or subject on the left hand side of the top line, and the year on the right hand side. The information from your field records can then be entered up, as briefly as possible in date order on the card (Fig. 16). The cards are filed in a box in alphabetical order of the species or subject—Accentor, Bathing, Brambling, Bullfinch, Chaffinch, Courtship, and so on. It is never too soon to start indexing your notes. In a year or two you are sure to want to know when you saw that magpie attacking a family of fledgling house sparrows, or that flock of fieldfares feeding on haws, and it is much easier if you index your daily observations from the start. Even in the unlikely event of your never discovering any new facts about any species of bird, your notes will still give you great pleasure in the years to come.

Fig. 17. A bird as those of us who are not artists might draw it

'come out the right shape', however much we try to alter it? The answer is because we began on a wrong foundation. To make an exact sketch you must understand the basic anatomy of a bird. In its simplest form a bird consists of two egg-shaped masses of tissue (the head and body) joined by a flexible neck.

SKETCHING BIRDS

'But, I never could draw!' is probably your exclamation on reading the title to this section. Everyone, even those who say they 'cannot draw', can make the rapid sketches that are so useful in describing birds and their behaviour, and which are so often much more effective than pages of written notes.

Let it be said at once that birds are not easy things to draw, but is there any subject that is? If you are quickly discouraged, then do not worry about it, but if you are determined to succeed, then in time your reward will be great.

The first drawing (Fig. 17), shows a bird as most of us might draw it. What is wrong? Why doesn't it

Fig. 18. Using the right foundations to draw a bird

For practice, begin by drawing an oval, and try to build up a bird on this sound foundation. Draw the head in front of the first shape, at the correct spot, and add the bird's neck and shoulders in a shapely manner. Now taper the rear of the body into a tail, remembering to 'streamline' it into the correct position. Now the legs. They are not just stuck inside the body like two match-sticks! Actually the leg-bones reach a long way into the body until they meet the main framework of the skeleton, for the joint just below the lower part of the body is really the ankle-joint, placed the same way round as that of a human being. Now continue the legs at an angle to the body, so that the bird looks as though it is well-balanced, and not propped up on stilts. After this, simply sketch in the position of the wings and feet and the outlines of the feathers, paying special attention to the position of the 'wrist' of the wings.

It is a great help to practise drawing a wing removed from a dead bird, carefully dried while it is fully extended, so that you can gain a better understanding of how the wing is constructed. Similarly, an examination of a mounted bird skeleton in a museum will help you with your sketching. Never copy other people's drawings. Study them and learn *how* the lines are made, by all means, and you will benefit thereby. Try your hand at sketching from photographs, for here you have what is, for our purposes, a picture of *life*, and by sketching from it you will learn much about construction, attitude,

Swallow

Young starling

Garden warbler

Robin

Fig. 19. Some field sketches of birds

light and shade. But do not spoil your work by making a mere imitation of a photographic print, complete in every detail. Look out for the essential lines and main features, and leave it at that.

Naturally, it is impossible for me to go into every detail of bird-sketching in one short section. My sole aim here is to help you make swift and objective records of interesting bird poses and actions. If you want to make a special study of the drawing of birds there are several good books available on the subject.

OBTAINING EXPERT HELP

It is always useful to know what other people are doing in the field of bird study and to seek their help and advice.

You should certainly join the Young Ornithologists' Club which is run by the Royal Society for the Protection of Birds. The club is open to everyone up to the age of eighteen years, and runs bird-watching outings and longer holiday courses, as well as organising interesting projects and surveys. Besides receiving the club's magazine which is packed with information on birds and bird-watching, you will also be put in touch with local adult bird-watchers who are able and willing to take out and help beginners.

You might also like to join your local county naturalists' trust, natural history society, field club or ornithological society. Any of these organizations will put you in touch with keen local bird-watchers, inform you where the local nature reserves or bird sanctuaries are, and generally help to make your bird study more enjoyable.

CHAPTER TWO

Attracting Birds to your Garden

The number and variety of birds in your garden can be greatly increased by providing them with food, nestboxes, cover for roosting, and water for both drinking and bathing.

Many species of birds can fend for themselves in the garden quite happily during the summer, but in the winter most of the natural sources of food give out, and unless you feed the birds they will either leave your garden to search for food elsewhere or die of starvation. In some northern countries many birds survive through the winter, only because they are fed by kindly people. This is certainly true with the great tit in northern Sweden, and may be the case with great and blue tits and some other species in Britain in a hard winter. Let us, therefore, first look at the ways in which we can help to see that the birds in our gardens get enough food to eat.

FOOD

Most birds soon cease to worry about the presence of humans in a garden. Some, such as robins and chaffinches, actually appear to enjoy Man's company, though no doubt their enjoyment is linked with the grubs and worms turned up by the gardener's spade. When the ground is hard with frost, or even when it is not, it is a great help to the birds to stir up the earthworms and other soil invertebrates.

Fig. 1. Some birds seem to enjoy man's company

Most gardens provide plenty of food during the summer months at least. Worms and insect larvae in the lawns and flower-beds, insect life amongst the leaves and branches, seeds of weeds and garden flowers, and sometimes, unhappily, fruit and vegetables too, are all eaten readily.

But you can do a lot to supplement nature's own rations, especially in winter when food is in short supply. Table scraps such as stale bread and cake crumbs, biscuit, egg, bacon, fat, meat, cereals and certain fruits and vegetables, if regularly provided, quickly attract such birds as starlings, sparrows, finches and blackbirds. If household scraps are not cleared up within twenty-four hours they should be removed otherwise they will act as a breeding-ground for germs.

Birds do have food preferences. The first choice of almost all birds is fat meat or bone marrow. Bacon or ham rinds and shredded suet are often easy to come by, but bones and meat should be cooked, or the birds may carry off lumps of meat which could spread disease.

The second favourite is bread and cheese—wholemeal bread is best because white bread so quickly becomes damp and 'doughy' and is inclined to swell inside the bird.

A third choice is nuts. Peanuts and cob-nuts are enjoyed by many birds, but the nuts will be carried away if they are not strung up on thread or placed in an open-work container of small mesh; these can be bought, but more will be said about this method of feeding later (page 36). Never feed salted nuts of any kind. Too much salt will kill some birds.

Coconuts attract a number of species, especially the tits. Cut the nut in half, having first drained off the milk, then make a hole through the base of each half and hang or nail each one upside down. If you fix them the other way up, water collects in the cup and the flesh of the nut goes mouldy. Do not, however, hang coconut in your garden during the breeding season since nestlings cannot digest it, and *never* feed dried, shredded (desiccated) coconut to birds, young or old; this really is dangerous, for it takes up moisture readily and can swell inside the bird and have

Fig. 2. Putting out a coconut for the birds

disastrous results. Remember that the majority of our garden birds feed their young on insects, and these are usually plentiful in the warmer months.

Soft fruit is eagerly eaten by many birds, hard fruit less so. It is sometimes possible to get waste and over-ripe fruit from greengrocers and street markets for nothing but the trouble of collecting it. Some raw vegetables such as potato, cabbage and roots are not acceptable, but cooked potatoes, especially if they are baked in their jackets and cut into pieces, are freely eaten. Raisins are a favourite, if somewhat expensive, food of many birds.

Many other foods are easily purchased. Wheat, oats and barley, as sold for poultry, are all cheap if bought in quite large quantities. They are popular with many species including not only the seed-eaters but also insectivorous birds such as the robin and the dunnock. Poultry feeding pellets, which are about the size of wheat grains, are eaten greedily by many birds.

The now famous 'Swoop' which can be bought in packets is a splendid all-round food as it contains seeds of various kinds, as well as nuts and specially processed fatty substances. You can make your own mixture if you like, from wheat, barley, kibbled maize, rolled oats, split or broken hemp, millet and buckwheat. To this can be added any weed seeds that you are able to collect.

If you are prepared to go to the trouble of cooking specially for the birds, you can offer them a variety of 'puddings' and other foods. One good, easy-to-make food is boiled rice or oatmeal mixed with melted fat. A similar mix can be made from stale bread or cake crumbs cemented with molten fat and a few currants.

It is particularly helpful to wedge small pieces of these two mixtures into crevices in trees, so that the smaller birds have their share before it is carried away by starlings, jackdaws, jays or magpies. Other favourite foods are pressure-cooked fish scraps or meat bones, and potatoes baked in their jackets and mixed with coarse oats, oatmeal or fat.

If you do not wish to go to the trouble of buying food for the birds, there are a number of wild foods which can be collected and stored. The so-called ants' eggs (actually these are the pupae and not the eggs) can be spooned from ant hills or the colonies that you may find under large stones. They will keep in an edible condition for many weeks if stored in the refrigerator until needed.

Hazel nuts, acorns, sweet chestnuts, horse chestnuts or 'conkers', and beech mast can usually be found in abundance at the right season, and they will last for many months if they are kept in a cool, dry place. Pine cones ripen in the early spring and they can yield useful quantities of edible seed if they are collected before their scales break apart. Place the cones in trays or boxes close to a radiator, where they will open, and allow the seeds to fall out.

Berries are more difficult to preserve, unless you have a deep-freeze at home; but they can be dried, like currants and sultanas, in a warm room until they have shrivelled, and then stored in a cool, dry place, away from the attacks of mice and mildew. Berries that can be treated in this way include elder, rowan (or mountain ash), hawthorn, holly, yew, ivy, cultivated honeysuckle, cotoneaster, berberis and pyracantha.

LIBRARY

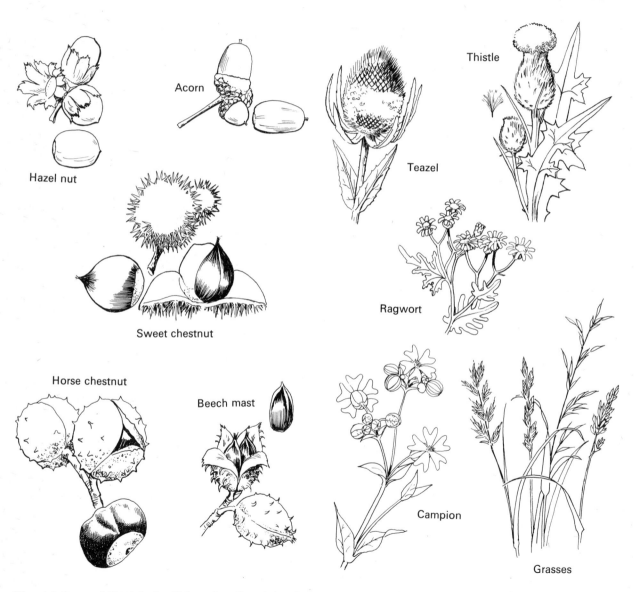

Fig. 3(a). Some wild bird foods which can be collected: hazel nuts, acorns, sweet chestnuts, horse chestnuts, beech mast, teazel, thistles (seeds), ragwort (seeds), campion (capsules containing seeds, not flowers), grasses

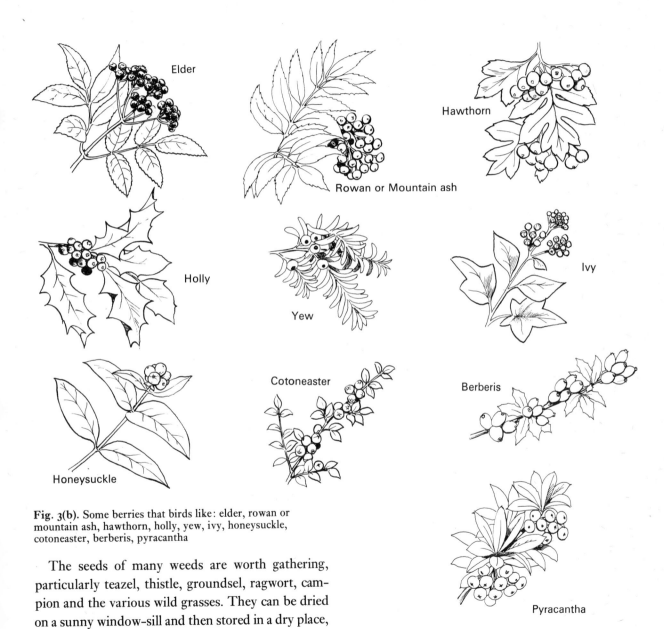

Fig. 3(b). Some berries that birds like: elder, rowan or mountain ash, hawthorn, holly, yew, ivy, honeysuckle, cotoneaster, berberis, pyracantha

The seeds of many weeds are worth gathering, particularly teazel, thistle, groundsel, ragwort, campion and the various wild grasses. They can be dried on a sunny window-sill and then stored in a dry place, out of reach of mice, until required.

Mealworms are almost essential if you wish to tame the birds in your garden so that they will feed from your hand. To a robin, a wriggling mealworm is irresistible and, if you are patient, this will almost certainly be the first bird to take food from your fingers. At the bird table, mealworms should be put in a small dish with steep sides which will reduce their chance of wriggling away.

Mealworms are not true worms, but the grubs of a small beetle, and you can either buy them at a pet shop (they are rather expensive), or rear your own.

The best way to breed mealworms is to take a large tin—a cake or biscuit tin is ideal, and half fill it with bran and one or two fingers of brown or wholemeal bread for them to feed on. Start the culture with a couple of hundred mealworms and place them in the bran together with a carrot or piece of damp cotton wool to provide moisture. Cover the tin with a lid made from zinc gauze or muslin. Keep the culture at about 26° to 30°C by placing it in an airing cupboard or on a radiator. The culture will take some time to

become established, but in due course the grubs, which are what the birds like best, will change into cream-coloured pupae and later still into beetles. Keep the beetles in the box, for they will lay eggs and then you will get a second generation of grubs without having to buy any more, and so on.

The only maintenance necessary is the occasional replacement of the bran when it becomes soiled. The old bran must be sifted first, though, to ensure that the eggs and young grubs are not thrown away. From time to time add another carrot or a new piece of damp cotton wool to provide water. Avoid excessive moisture or harmful moulds will grow; if they appear, change the tin and bran, and start again.

BIRD TABLES

It is very instructive, and sometimes amusing, to have a bird table within sight of the sitting room window so that you can watch the behaviour of the birds while feeding. Almost any bowl, dish, tray or box lid will serve as a temporary table. It is, however, easy to make one that is efficient yet simple, durable without being unpleasant to look at.

Do not make the feeding tray too small. An area of about 2,000 cm^2 is probably the most convenient size. A piece of plywood, 1·5 to 2·5 cm thick, and of outdoor quality, will stand up to the weather for a number of years whereas many of the soft woods will warp, twist or crack quite rapidly. To prevent the food from blowing or rolling off, a narrow rim of beading projected 2 to 3 cm high should be fitted; it should not be

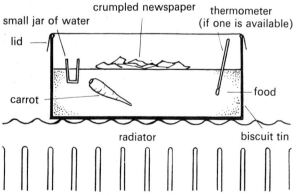

Fig. 4. Breeding mealworms

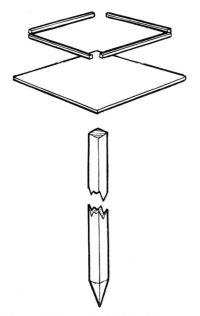
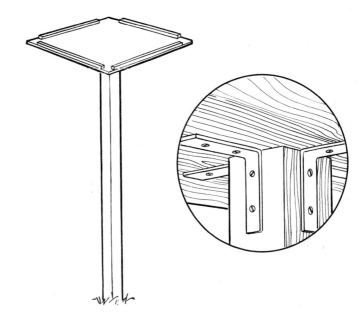

Fig. 5. Making a simple bird table

continuous as one or two gaps must be left, each about 2 cm wide to allow rainwater to run off (see Fig. 5).

Some people simply screw the table top to the wood of a window ledge so that the birds are really close to the observer in the room as they feed. One disadvantage of this is that the glass may become soiled by the splashing of rain and the birds' activities in feeding. Another is that the shy birds will not readily come as close to the house as this, and some birds, seeing themselves in the glass, waste much time and energy, and often injure themselves, in violently attacking their own reflection, mistaking it for a rival bird of the same sex.

It is therefore, more suitable for all concerned to suspend the table from a tree or to make it free

standing. If the table is to be hung up, it is only necessary to fasten screw eyes and strings on it (Fig. 6), otherwise, fit the table top onto a smooth

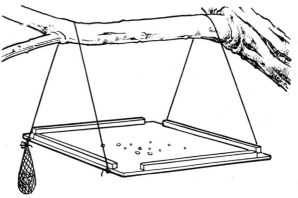

Fig. 6. Another way of fixing a simple bird table

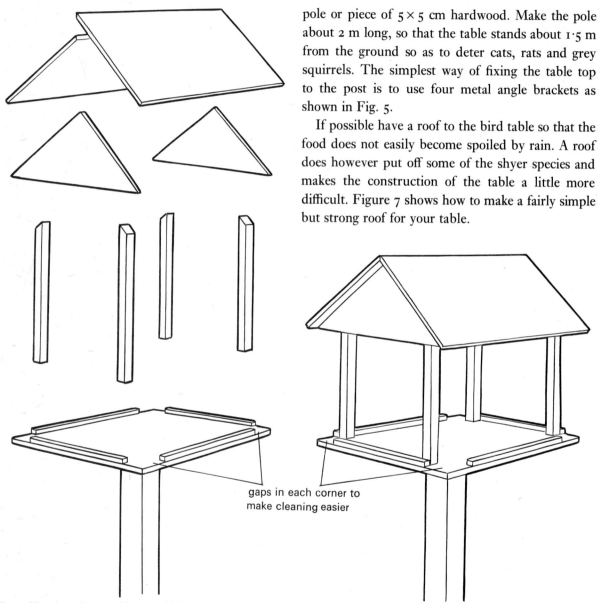

pole or piece of 5×5 cm hardwood. Make the pole about 2 m long, so that the table stands about 1·5 m from the ground so as to deter cats, rats and grey squirrels. The simplest way of fixing the table top to the post is to use four metal angle brackets as shown in Fig. 5.

If possible have a roof to the bird table so that the food does not easily become spoiled by rain. A roof does however put off some of the shyer species and makes the construction of the table a little more difficult. Figure 7 shows how to make a fairly simple but strong roof for your table.

gaps in each corner to
make cleaning easier

Fig. 7. How to make a roof for your bird table

If you can, place the table a few metres from some 'cover', such as a hedge or some bushes. By doing this you will be providing a wind-break and also a place to which the birds can quickly retreat if cats appear. The shelter provided will soon be used by many birds which are waiting there for a chance to go to the table.

If you wish to have more than one bird table in your garden, effective but not very hard-wearing suspended tables can be made from seed trays as shown in Fig. 8a. If two potato or tomato trays are fixed together and suspended, as shown in Fig. 8b, then the upper tray will provide a table at which all birds can feed, while the food in the lower tray will only be used by the smaller birds such as the tits.

Do not forget that some birds prefer to feed on the ground and will not go to the bird table unless they are extremely hungry. These ground-feeding species can be catered for by putting the food on an old tray at the foot of a hedge or at the base of a tree. The tray can then be taken in at night so that it does not attract mice and rats.

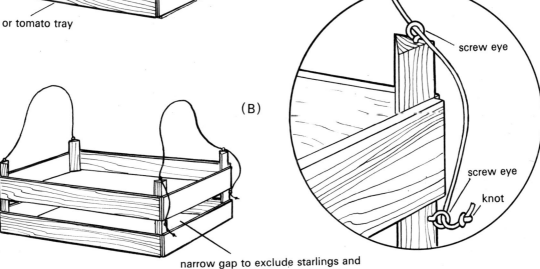

(A)

potato or tomato tray

(B)

string

screw eye

screw eye

knot

narrow gap to exclude starlings and other large birds

Fig. 8. Making a bird table from potato or tomato trays

PLATE I. Tits feeding on peanuts in a food basket

PLATE II. A covered bird table

FEEDING DEVICES

Birds are not orderly guests, and it is annoying to see starlings, jackdaws, gulls and other large birds gobbling up or carrying off food as soon as it is put out. This cannot be prevented altogether, but it can be reduced by hanging up meat, fat and bread scraps in a wire netting container. The R.S.P.B. make an excellent, inexpensive food basket which can also be used for nuts. A good, cheap substitute is the small plastic net bags in which nuts and fruit can be bought. Neatly cut one end off the bag and remove the contents. Take care not to tear the bag. Fill it with bird food, being careful not to overfill, and tie the top with string. Leave enough spare string to suspend the bag from the underside of the bird table or from the branch of a tree. Small birds will cling to the basket or bag and extract the food gradually, but large birds which attempt to do so will not have much success.

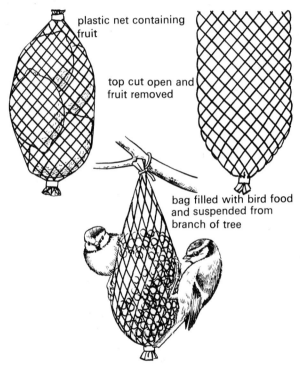

Fig. 9. Making a food basket from a small plastic net bag

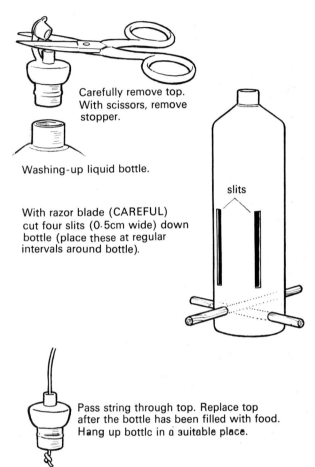

Carefully remove top. With scissors, remove stopper.

Washing-up liquid bottle.

With razor blade (CAREFUL) cut four slits (0·5cm wide) down bottle (place these at regular intervals around bottle).

slits

Pass string through top. Replace top after the bottle has been filled with food. Hang up bottle in a suitable place.

Fig. 10. Making a food basket from an old washing-up liquid bottle

It is some years now since Mr. H. Mortimer Batten invented the tit feeding bell, but this device is still very useful. An alternative is any smooth bell-shaped container. A half coconut or a flower pot are both excellent and if hung, mouth downwards, they will defeat starlings and other ground feeding species. The container is filled with food, and either a lid of 1 cm wire mesh is fitted, or the food is held in place by hot melted fat poured in and allowed to set before the container is suspended mouth downwards (Fig. 12). It will be visited by tits, nuthatches, woodpeckers and other climbing experts.

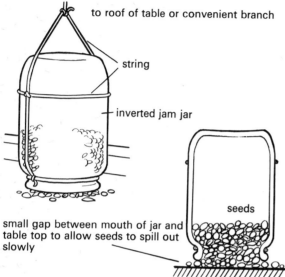

to roof of table or convenient branch

string

inverted jam jar

seeds

small gap between mouth of jar and table top to allow seeds to spill out slowly

Fig. 11. A seed hopper for the bird table

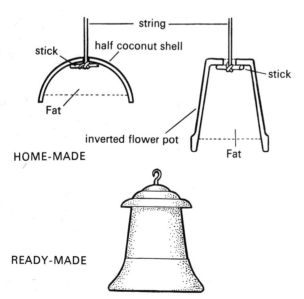

string

stick   half coconut shell

Fat

stick

inverted flower pot

Fat

HOME-MADE

READY-MADE

Fig. 12. Feeding bells

WHEN TO STOP FEEDING

In feeding birds in a town garden where the supply of natural foods is limited, the bird lover is liable to make his birds dependent upon him for their regular supply of food, and if this is suddenly cut off some hardship is created. It is particularly cruel to cut off the supply of food in winter and, if you have to go away during the bad weather, ask a neighbour or friend to continue your work of feeding the birds in your garden.

In the spring the number of birds visiting your garden will probably be reduced as the winter visitors to this country fly north to their summer quarters. The resident birds come less eagerly as more natural foods become available in garden and countryside. If you live in the country or in a fairly rural suburb you can considerably reduce the amount of food you put out. A little wheat and seed will encourage the finches but if you continue to feed bread and fat you will find some birds will overeat themselves, feed their nestlings with an unsuitable diet and neglect natural insect foods which are essential for young birds. There is another good reason for not lavishly feeding birds in the spring and summer: you are making them earn their own keep by helping to reduce the large quantities of caterpillars and other garden pests which are most active at this time of year. If the weather suddenly turns very dry or very cold, you may increase the ration, but generally the birds' behaviour is a good guide in deciding whether they are really hungry or not.

WATER

As great an attraction to birds as food is water, especially in built up areas where there is little or no surface water in dry weather.

Water is needed for both drinking and bathing. Birds bathe in summer and winter alike, no matter how cold it is. In my garden, starlings in particular are always eager to bathe even when it has been necessary to break thick ice to allow them to do so. If birds are to fly properly and maintain their body temperature, feathers have to be kept in good condition, and before they can start to preen properly, birds must bathe. Incidentally some birds actually bathe in flight; swallows and swifts dive down to the water and take a quick dip as they flash by.

Fig. 13. Providing water for the birds

Where space is restricted, a shallow drinking bowl will have to do, about 10 cm wide and deep enough to hold 2 to 3 cm of water. This must be changed daily and the bowl cleaned of droppings; sterilize the bowl with a solution of household disinfectant at intervals, but make sure that it is thoroughly rinsed before it is refilled with water.

If more room is available then larger containers can be used. Whatever vessel you use, make sure that it is not too slippery as the birds must be able to get a good grip. An upturned dustbin lid is very suitable and even an old frying pan is better than a fancy bird bath surrounded by gnomes, pixies and plaster frogs. Alternatively an old sink can be let into the ground so that about 3 cm of the sides are above ground level. Place a couple of large stones in it so that the birds can get at the water.

The best thing is a larger pool in the ground, constructed in a position where it can be watched from indoors. It can be stocked with water plants gathered from local ditches and ponds or obtained from a pet shop or horticultural dealer. If the pool is large enough, small fish, newts, toads, frogs, water snails and insects can be introduced. It is not unknown for a heron or kingfisher to make an early morning visit to a garden pond. A large pool should always have a shallow region, not only for small water animals, but also for birds to walk in and out to bathe and paddle.

To prevent water from the pond from draining into the porous soil, the pond must be lined with a waterproof material of some sort. Polythene sheeting is the cheapest and best for small pools. It can be obtained in a suitable blue or green shade, and if carefully laid on a smooth foundation it will last indefinitely. Disguise the lining by putting down a layer of clean sand and a little peat, and by overlapping the edge with turf and flowering plants (Fig. 14).

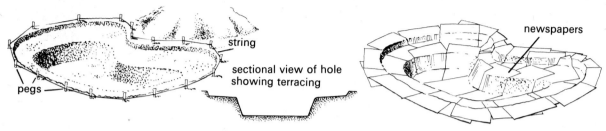

Before digging the pool it is best to mark out the ground with strings. There should be a shallow shelf all the way round as birds will not drink or bathe in deep water. Level and firm the bottom and sides of the hole.

Remove as many stones as possible from the sides and bottom of the hole and then line it with many sheets of newspaper to prevent sharp stones puncturing the polythene. If the weather is windy wet the newspapers to prevent them blowing away.

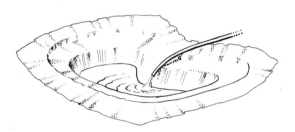

Line the hole with polythene sheeting, leaving a big overlap all round, and fill the pool. You can calculate the area of polythene needed for your pool by this simple formula
Length of polythene: length of pool (at surface) + Twice the greatest depth + 75cm
width of polythene: width of pool (at surface) +twice the greatest depth + 75cm

The polythene round the edge of the pool is covered with paving stones or turfs.
The pool can now be planted. The plants should be potted in special containers which look rather like wastepaper baskets or in buckets or tins with many holes punched in them.

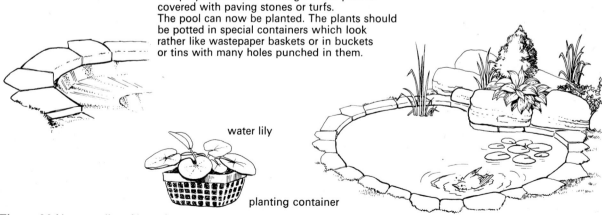

Fig. 14. Making a small garden pool

One word of warning: when providing drinking and bathing facilities for birds do not put water close to any place where cats might lurk. Birds get very excited about their bath-time and may forget to keep a proper watch.

How to keep water from freezing in winter is a problem not easily solved. If you have a small bird-bath in the garden, a night-light in a tin or an inverted flower-pot beneath the bowl will prevent the water from freezing, unless temperatures fall very low (Fig. 15). For larger areas of water it will be necessary to break the ice whenever it freezes. If there are fish in the water do not do this with a hammer since the vibrations may injure the fish. Instead, lower the bottom of a hot kettle onto the ice until it melts. A large rubber ball floating on the water will sometimes help to prevent the whole surface from freezing over.

Whatever you do, do not add anything to the water. For salt to be effective, so much would have to be used that no land bird would take a second sip. Glycerine is sticky, and birds hate getting their beaks in a mess, whilst anti-freeze would poison them. There is, unfortunately, no substitute for a little hard work and trouble.

Fig. 15. Using a night-light to prevent the birds' water from freezing

As with food, having attracted birds to your garden with water during the summer when it may be plentiful, you have a duty to maintain the supply during the winter.

DUST BATHS

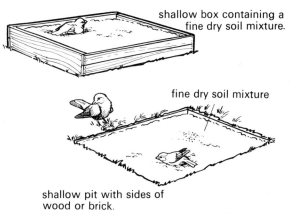

shallow box containing a fine dry soil mixture.

fine dry soil mixture

shallow pit with sides of wood or brick.

Fig. 16. A dust bath for the birds

Some birds like to wallow in dust and dry-clean their plumage of parasites and scale. To cater for this, you need a shallow box containing a fine dry soil mixture. In large gardens a shallow pit, with sides of wood or brick, can be constructed. The box or pit should be sited in a warm sunny spot, preferably facing south. A suitable mixture for the dust bath consists of equal parts of sharp sand, soil and well-sifted ash. Ant-heaps provide excellent fine crumbly soil. A little pyrethrum insect powder can be scattered in the dust bath from time to time to help destroy any of the parasites that the bathing birds may leave behind.

Having constructed the bath, it is a good idea to bait the surface with a few grains of wheat to get the birds interested. Some birds have the curious habit of inserting ants in their feathers as they dust bathe, and a study of this habit is described on page 89.

NESTING MATERIAL

Some birds in town areas find difficulty in obtaining suitable nesting material, so a supply of nesting material provides a great attraction to them, and in fact to country birds as well, during the spring and early summer.

Collect together as much as you can of things like dry hay, dried moss, knitting wool cut into pieces a few centimetres long, sheep's wool which is often to be found sticking to a barbed wire fence, dog and cat combings, carpet fluff, chicken feathers and put them into a large string bag. The bags in which onions and Brussels sprouts are sent to greengrocers' shops

Fig. 17. Providing nesting material for the birds

are ideal. Hang the bag from a stout branch of a tree or from a clothes line, and insert one or more sticks to act as perches through the lower part of the bag (Fig. 17).

By watching where the birds take the nesting material you will soon be able to find the nests in your area.

BIRD GARDENING

The term *bird gardening* was invented some years ago by that great naturalist, broadcaster, lecturer and author, the late Maxwell Knight, who wrote a book with that title.

The phrase is used here in a more limited sense to refer to plants that you can introduce into your garden in order to attract a greater variety of bird species.

Many birds prefer the seeds of weeds to those of cultivated garden flowers, but apart from the fact that many weeds are unsightly, it is not advisable to encourage them in your garden or you may be in trouble with your neighbours and sometimes, indeed, the law. You can, however, help the birds by planting seed-bearing plants, particularly sunflowers and michaelmas daisies, and by not being in too much of a hurry to cut down the dead flowering stems until the birds have had their fill of the seeds.

During hard weather large numbers of birds will visit your garden if you have planted berry-bearing shrubs. Thrushes and blackbirds especially are attracted to gardens with berries and in the so-called 'waxwing winters', the years when these handsome crested birds invade the British Isles from the Continent, a good supply of berries could bring these together with other unusual and exotic visitors, even to a town garden. The list of suitable berries is almost endless, but birds are especially fond of the fruits of cotoneaster, japonica, berberis, elder, rowan, holly, hawthorn, pyracantha, cherry, viburnum, stanvaesia, ivy, guelder rose and cultivated honeysuckle.

From the gardener's point of view it is rather unforunate that the garden which birds like best is one that is not too tidy. An overgrown patch of bushes and brambles is excellent, so too is a weedy area. However, you can do much by creating variety with as many different plants and shrubs as possible. A number of shrubs and creepers are satisfactory as windbreaks, cover and nesting sites. Holly, hawthorn and blackthorn are good all-rounders, and also produce edible berries. Yew, box and privet hedges form useful windbreaks and are popular for nesting. Creepers of all kinds, including ivy, cotoneaster, forsythia and jasmine provide nesting sites.

Most gardens these days have a lawned area and one thing that must be avoided at all costs is the use of chemical worm-killers. Worms can undoubtedly be a nuisance on a lawn by producing unsightly 'casts', but if you attempt to poison the worms you will probably, without realising it, poison some of the large number of birds which eat earthworms.

Aim to have a garden which, for your own sake as well as that of the birds, is not wind-swept, and which provides a variety of berries in winter and ample nest sites in spring. The question of nestboxes is discussed in the next section.

NESTBOXES

An excellent way to attract and conserve bird life is to provide nestboxes in the garden. Most hole-nesting species will nest in these, but in small gardens the most likely species are great and blue tits, spotted flycatchers, nuthatches, robins, and the inevitable house sparrows and even starlings if the entrance hole of the boxes is large enough. In larger or rural gardens, coal and marsh tits, tree sparrows, redstarts and pied flycatchers may be added to the list of nesters.

PLATE III. A simple nestbox

PLATE IV. Marsh tit feeding her young

PLATE V. Robin at nest in an open fronted nestbox

There are basically two kinds of nestbox. One is a closed box, or sometimes a cylinder, with a small entrance hole; this is favoured by tits, redstarts, sparrows, starlings, nuthatches and pied flycatchers. The other type is an open box tray or ledge from which the sitting bird can look out. Robins, pied wagtails and spotted flycatchers prefer this type.

These two kinds of nestbox are not difficult to make, although, if you prefer it, you can buy excellent

nestboxes from the Royal Society for the Protection of Birds. For the closed box, Figure 18a shows how to cut a piece of unplaned softwood board such as cedar, or deal which is much cheaper. The plank should be 130 cm long, 15 cm wide and 2 cm thick. The cut marked by the two crosses is best made by holding the saw at an angle, so making two sloping edges, one for the front and another for the roof. These will ensure that where the roof touches the back of the box,

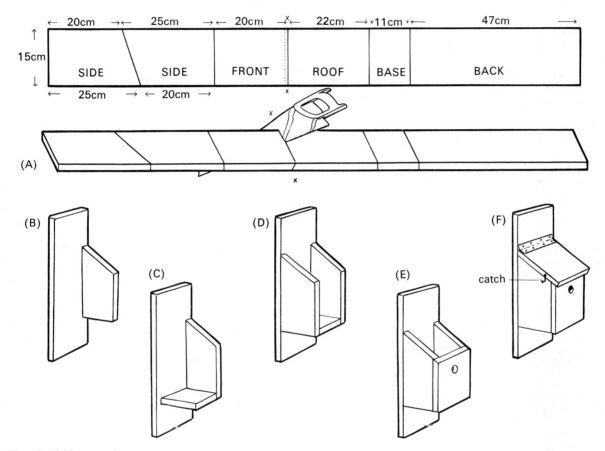

Fig. 18. Making a nestbox

and where the front touches the roof, a close fit will not allow rain to penetrate.

Draw the entrance hole on the front, about 5 cm below the roof, using a pair of compasses. Cut out the hole with a drill or brace and bit. If neither of these tools is available, make a small hole with a gimlet or bradawl, and then enlarge it with a chisel or cut round the circle with a coping saw.

If you want tits to use the box, the entrance hole should be not more than 3 cm in diameter. For larger birds, such as sparrows and redstarts, the hole should be not more than 4 cm in diameter. In the case of starlings, the box itself must be larger: 30 cm long with base 25 cm by 25 cm, with a hole 5 cm in diameter.

To return to our original box, it is now ready to

assemble. Begin by nailing one side to the back (Fig. 18b), using thin nails about 3 cm long. Then hold the base in position, and nail it to the back and side (Fig. 18c). Now go on to nail the other side to the back and base (Fig. 18d). Place the front in position and see that it does not project too far, using the roof to check this. Then nail the front in position (Fig. 18e).

For a hinge, use a strip of waterproof material, 15 cm long and 5 cm wide. Rubber, particularly a piece of old car inner tube, is ideal, but waterproof canvas and leather can also be used. Fix this in position using a dozen copper tacks. Finally, fit a catch on either side of the box to hold the lid firmly in place in the strongest of winds (Fig. 18f).

If you have used deal or some other untreated softwood, paint the outside of the box with a preservative, such as cuprinol.

Roofed nestboxes of the open entrance type are made in a similar way, but the front is only 10 cm long and is fitted as shown in Fig. 19, and there is no need for a hinged lid.

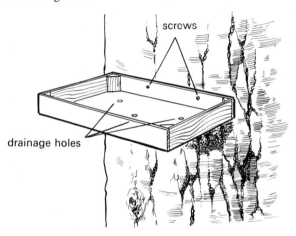

Fig. 20. A wooden tray nestbox

Another very simple nestbox is a plain wooden tray with a few holes drilled in the bottom, for drainage (Fig. 20). This may be used by the same species as the roofed box with the open entrance (robin, pied wagtail, spotted flycatcher), or the blackbird. If the tray is fastened high up on a beam or ledge in an out-building, it may be taken over by swallows.

A perch is not necessary for any of these nestboxes, in fact it provides an open invitation to predators to sit and harass the owners. Similarly, see that the box is firmly secured and away from branches or other possible foot-holds for enemies.

Birds begin looking for nest-sites some weeks before they actually begin to build. You must therefore put up the box in good time, not later than the middle

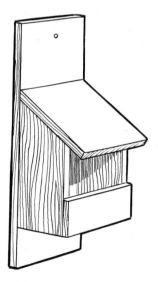

Fig. 19. Nestbox of the open entrance type

of March for most species, although if nesting holes are scarce in your area, there is a possibility that they may be snatched up as nest-sites later than this.

If your box is to be put in a place where it is liable to human disturbance, then it is essential that it be fixed at least 3 m from the ground. Remember also to put the box out of reach of cats. The closed type of nestbox should be firmly fixed to a tree, fence or wall so that it cannot fall down or vibrate in high winds. Where there is no natural shade available, the box should face away from the midday sun. An easterly aspect is best. If you are fixing the box to a tree, do not put it on a part of the trunk where there is a green band. This indicates that water regularly trickles down the trunk, making it a bad site for a box. If the nestbox is tilted forward slightly, sun and driving rain will be kept out. Open-fronted boxes should be sited on a wall which is covered with a creeper or shrub; open-topped boxes can be fastened on to the trunks or branches of trees, on creeper-covered walls, or on beams in outbuildings. Do not bother to put nesting material in the box, as any birds that wish to take up residence almost always collect their own material, and will build on top of your lining.

As well as nestboxes there are other, cheaper, nest-sites that you can provide for the birds. An old, lidless kettle is a favourite nesting site of robins, wrens and flycatchers. It should be firmly fixed on its side in a hedge, in a bank or against a wall. The spout can be removed altogether or left, but the opening should be placed downwards to allow water to drain out. In this case a little dried moss or hay put inside may well encourage tenants.

Fig. 21. An old kettle as a nest site for the birds

Large flower pots, old jugs and small boxes can also be discreetly hidden in a bank or on a wall in thick supporting vegetation, but they must have good drainage holes to prevent flooding in heavy rain.

One of the great advantages of artificial nest sites is that they provide a golden opportunity for you to follow the progress of the nesting birds. Unfortunately it is all too easy to allow your enthusiasm to run away with you and cause the parent birds to desert the nest, or frighten the young away. To prevent this sort of thing from happening, you should never touch the eggs, young or sitting birds, however briefly. Look at the nest no more than once a day, and preferably less often than this, and then spend as little time as possible there. If the nestbox has a lid, replace it gently.

Try not to visit the nest while the bird is sitting on her eggs and never go to the nest when the young are more than half-grown (if you do not know how long it takes for any bird to become fully fledged, you can check this in a reference book). If the young birds leave the nest before they are ready, they will be snatched up by a cat, grey squirrel, or some other predator.

Nestboxes require very little attention. At the end of summer they should be emptied out and the old nesting material burned. Old nests usually contain the eggs or larvae of bird parasites such as fleas, ticks, lice and mites which pass the winter in this form and then prey on a new generation of birds next spring. To make doubly sure that these pests are destroyed, sprinkle the bottom of the box with a little insecticide powder containing pyrethrum or derris (these are not poisonous to birds) and cover it with a little fresh hay or moss. Many boxes are used for roosting during the winter, so it may be necessary to give another spring-clean before the next nesting season begins.

Wooden nestboxes will last longer if given a coat of preservative such as creosote or cuprinol each year. But this treatment should never be carried out later than September or October for the birds will not use the boxes for roosting or nesting until the strong smell has worn off.

For those who wish to go more deeply into the interesting business of making nestboxes for a greater variety of bird species, the British Trust for Ornithology publishes an inexpensive booklet, **Nest-boxes** that gives information on making boxes for swifts, house martins, jackdaws, kestrels, tawny owls and many other species.

CHAPTER THREE

Waifs, Strays and Casualties

HAND-REARING ORPHANED BIRDS

Every spring and summer you will probably come across stranded fledglings that are too young to fend for themselves. All too often, however, these nestlings have not been deserted at all but, having left the nest, are being fed by their parents on the ground until they are able to fly.

Young birds, like human babies, call out when they are hungry, and parent birds, like human parents, are well trained to hear these sounds even if they are some distance away. So if you do find a young bird that cannot fly, put it in a safe place, out of reach of cats, for its mother and father to find and feed.

No nestling should be removed altogether until you are absolutely certain that both parents are dead or for some other reason unable to care for it. Hand-rearing a young bird takes a lot of time, trouble and patience since the nestling needs frequent attention. Unless you are prepared to devote the necessary care to it, or can find someone to do it for you, then the merciful step of painless destruction should be taken. Immediate action is essential if you decide to rear the young birds, for nestlings rapidly weaken unless they are given warmth and food quickly.

Warmth can be provided in the form of a cardboard box, deep enough to prevent the bird from climbing out when it gets bigger. Relate the size of the box to the bird that is being reared—a shoe box will do for a

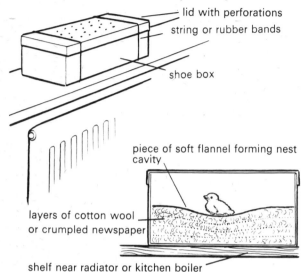

lid with perforations
string or rubber bands
shoe box

piece of soft flannel forming nest cavity

layers of cotton wool
or crumpled newspaper

shelf near radiator or kitchen boiler

small pellet of food

Fig. 1. A box for an orphaned nestling

Fig. 2. Feeding a nestling

sparrow or chaffinch; jackdaws and larger birds will need a bigger box. The box should contain several layers of cotton wool or crumpled newspaper, with a piece of soft flannel on top. No extra heat is necessary as long as the box is kept in a fairly warm and draught-free room at about 16°C. A shelf near the kitchen boiler or near a radiator is ideal.

Until the nestling is partly feathered, keep the lid on the box (having first punched air-holes in it), held tightly in place with string or rubber bands. The lid not only discourages cats and human intruders, but also keeps the bird in the dark, helping to quieten it.

Until a more suitable food can be obtained—and one always seems to come across these waifs and strays at the most inconvenient times—moistened bread (preferably brown or wholemeal) will do, but for two or three feeds only. Take a small pellet of

bread, mount it on the end of a blunt match-stick and push it, gently, well down in the bird's gullet. If the bird gapes its mouth wide open this is easy to do, if not the beak should be gently forced open with the finger and thumb nails. The bird will soon learn to gape after two or three of these forced feeds.

For regular feeding of the smaller insect-eating birds, up to the size of a blackbird, a paste can be made from crushed biscuit—oatmeal biscuits are ideal—mixed with a little hard-boiled egg yolk and water (not milk since this quickly goes sour). The paste should be firm enough for it to be rolled into pellets about the size of a pea. Make fresh paste each day and keep it in a cool place, otherwise it may cause the bird internal upsets. Give two or three of these small pellets each meal (depending upon the bird's appetite), and feed about every hour from dawn until dusk. If you cannot get up really early, then you must be prepared to work some other 16 hour day. I did warn you that hand-rearing is hard work!

As well as the pellet, and sometimes as a change instead of it, give the bird a few tiny pieces of chopped-up earthworm or mealworm, or even small moths and flies, every other meal or so. Special insectivorous bird foods can be bought from pet-shops which are graded according to the size of the bird for which they are intended.

Young seed-eaters such as sparrows, finches and buntings may be fed on biscuit meal with some added cod-liver oil biscuit and a little egg; again a fresh supply should be made each day.

Hand-reared birds require a small amount of water each day and this can be given by dipping the little finger into a dish of water and carefully letting the drop at the end of the finger run down the bird's throat.

When the bird is fully fledged, a pot of food should be kept in the cage to encourage it to start feeding by itself. However, you should not stop hand-feeding until you are absolutely certain that the young bird can feed itself; even then, it may be necessary to hand-feed occasionally to ensure that the young bird is getting enough food for healthy growth.

During the process of hand-rearing, the question of cleanliness must, of course, be attended to, for if droppings are not removed regularly they can soon result in great discomfort and sometimes even the death of the fledgling. The droppings are produced in a kind of 'sac' made of a tough jelly-like substance, and are easily removed with a pair of blunt tweezers. If the young bird's hindquarters become fouled, they should be gently cleaned using a piece of cotton wool dipped in tepid water. If there are any signs of soreness, a little Vaseline should be gently rubbed in. Soiled nesting material should be removed as soon as possible.

All young birds require a certain amount of exercise from the time their feathers appear. The easiest way

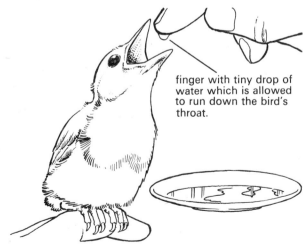

finger with tiny drop of water which is allowed to run down the bird's throat.

Fig. 3. Giving water to a hand-reared bird

The fledgling bird is placed on the hand or finger and the hand gently raised up and down. This will cause the bird to flap its wings

Fig. 4. Exercising an orphaned fledgling

to exercise the wings is to place the bird on your finger or hand and gently raise your hand up and down. This will cause the bird to flap its wings. The legs can be exercised either by letting the bird walk about the room, while you are there to keep an eye on it, or by putting it in a roomy cage in which it can move about freely. Later on the bird will need flying practice and this should be done in a room with the curtains drawn, or the bird will fly towards the windows and injure itself.

It is not possible to mention here all the other types of birds that one may be asked to rear, but mention will be made of two of the common ones. Members of the crow family such as rooks, jackdaws and magpies can be fed on the paste already described plus chopped worm for the first week or so, but after that they should be given minced raw meat mixed with table scraps and, in addition, whole earthworms, beetles, grubs of all kinds, grasshoppers, and any other insects which are available. With the birds of prey: the hawks and owls, the technique of hand-rearing is somewhat different. From the beginning the nestling is fed on flesh of some kind, as well as beetles and earthworms. At least a small quantity of fur and feather should be given with the flesh, because all the birds of prey regularly cast up the undigested remains of their food in the form of a pellet (see Chapter 4).

Eventually when your bird has passed through its infancy, you must prepare for the day when it can be released. It is in fact illegal to keep one of the vast majority of wild birds in captivity unless it is injured, sick or orphaned. Even so, the bird must be released as soon as it is well enough to fend for itself. This means that you must gradually make the bird less dependent on you by giving it more and more opportunity to practise flying and by enabling it to recognize, find and hunt for food. When the bird is able to do all of these things efficiently, you will be able to let it go and have the satisfaction of knowing that you have played a part in helping to conserve our bird life.

EXHAUSTED AND STARVING BIRDS

Sometimes you will come across an exhausted or starving bird that has been the victim of bad weather conditions whilst on migration. You are more likely to find such birds however, during a long spell of very cold, snowy weather when all natural supplies of food have been cut off.

The starving or exhausted bird should be put in a wire-fronted wooden box of suitable size containing a perch. Keep it at a comfortable indoor temperature and give the bird suitable food and water. If the bird was found towards the end of the day, put it in artificial light for a few hours so that it can see to feed. For seed-eaters, the mixture sold for budgerigars will do, whilst for the small insect-eaters, special foods are available from dealers, although any small live food to be found in the garden, or mealworms, will do. Mealworms are rather fatty and hard to digest, and no more than six a day should be given.

In the case of the larger birds you must consult a

good reference book for details of the food suitable for that particular species.

In emergencies, bread-and-milk, sultanas and a dish of water will be accepted readily by any bird, large or small.

As soon as the bird is fit and strong again, it can be released once the weather has improved.

INJURED BIRDS

If you find an injured bird, the first task is to discover the nature of its injuries. It is then necessary to decide whether it has any chance of recovery, and if so whether you are prepared to care for a crippled bird permanently. Otherwise the bird should be handed over to one of the animal rescue societies such as the R.S.P.C.A. or P.D.S.A., or painlessly destroyed at once. In any case, you must not be too disappointed if the bird dies. It has probably had a severe shock and may have been injured internally. Warmth, food, water and quiet are the first essential, especially if the bird has been picked up in cold weather.

When the bird has had a chance to rest and feed, then you can set about treating its injuries, although in many cases slightly injured birds will heal themselves if given warmth, food, water and quiet conditions, without the need for surgical treatment.

Wounds should be treated by carefully cutting the feathers away from the affected area with scissors and bathing the wounds with tepid water. Never use antiseptics.

Broken wings are as hard to cure as they are common.

Using sharp scissors, gently cut short all the large primary feathers on the affected wing. This will put the wing out of action until the next moult, by which time the wing will probably have healed itself. Splints of match-sticks and sticky tape can be used if one has the necessary skill and nimble fingers.

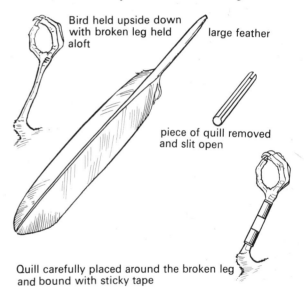

Fig. 5. Putting a splint on a broken leg

Broken legs can be treated if the break is in the lower part of the leg, well away from a joint. A good splint can be made by splitting open the quill of a large feather such as that of a goose or swan, partly enclosing the broken limb with a length of this (Fig. 5), and binding the whole with sticky tape. Broken thigh bones seldom heal successfully.

Keep the injured bird quiet in a covered cage fitted with several short tree branches as perches, and with a supply of water and suitable food.

OILED SEA BIRDS

Oiling is one of the worst by-products of our civili-
zation, and particularly affects those sea birds such as
razorbills, puffins, guillemots and gannets which have
to swim or dive through the oily surface of the water.
The oil destroys the texture of the feathers so that the
bird suffers from the cold and wet. The bird cannot
hunt for food, and when it tries to preen itself it may
swallow some of the oil which could have serious
results. An oiled bird is, therefore, likely to be
starved, cold and sick when it is eventually washed
ashore.

If the bird is badly oiled, thin and weak, it should be
painlessly destroyed. If it is lightly oiled, it has a slim
chance of survival if it is kept warm, taken to shelter
quickly, and expert help is sought.

When the Torrey Canyon oil tanker ran aground
off Land's End in Cornwall, seriously polluting the
sea and beaches, the R.S.P.C.A. and other helpers
rescued 8,000 oiled sea birds, but the total number of
birds that survived treatment and were later released
was probably only about 100. Until we know more
about solving the problems of treating oiled sea birds,
badly affected victims will have to be destroyed.
Slightly oiled birds should be passed on to one of the
animal rescue societies as quickly as possible, and the
local police station will usually be able to suggest
someone who can help you.

CHAPTER FOUR

Collections

We are all collectors at heart. The desire to collect anything from matchbox labels to antiques is present in all of us, but naturalists in general and ornithologists in particular, will be well advised never to collect solely in order to have *more* of something than someone else.

A jumble of tattered and unidentified specimens looks untidy and is scientifically worthless. A good, well-balanced and properly labelled collection can be both pleasing to the eye and very instructive. The point I am trying to make is really this: do not collect for the sake of collecting, and do not collect things without any thought of the ultimate use to which the collection will be put. A collection may only be justified as a necessary object of instruction or reference for future work or if the things collected can be taken without unnecessary injury to the individual birds or the species concerned.

This point brings us to the delicate subject of the collection of birds' eggs. Some people maintain that it is downright cruel to take the eggs of any bird, while others uphold the view that if collecting is carried out sensibly and kept within reasonable limits, no great harm is done. These people give strength to their argument by suggesting that even if a whole clutch of eggs is taken, the hen bird will probably lay a second clutch to compensate for her loss. Unfortunately for this argument, the collector is in no position to know whether he is taking the first clutch, or a second clutch laid to make good the loss of the first.

Let me say right away that I am against collections of birds' eggs of any kind. Most collections made by beginners are worthless, and it is difficult to avoid doing harm in amassing them. Furthermore, the Protection of Birds Act 1954 makes it a punishable offence for anyone, save those few trained scientists properly authorised by licence, to take the eggs of wild birds, or to interfere with the birds themselves, or the nests while they are in use.

The items described in the following pages are all suitable for collection and they will involve no danger to the species, or cruelty if they are collected properly. What is more, these items can teach you a lot about the living bird, which after all is our real object of study. In particular they help to show various ways in which birds are adapted to the lives they lead.

BIRD PELLETS

The study of bird pellets is absorbing and instructive since it gives valuable clues to the food eaten by various species of birds.

Pellets are the remains of food items which cannot be digested and disposed of in the ordinary way, and are coughed up and ejected via the beak. More than 60 species are known to produce pellets like this and they include not only the birds of prey such as owls and hawks, but also crows, gulls, and a number of small birds such as robins and flycatchers.

In other words, a pellet is a packet which consists

PLATE VI. A Tawny Owl

of a binding material which varies from fur and feathers, to sand, fish-scales and bits of grass and moss; inside this packet there may be the hard parts of insects, the claws and bones of birds and mammals, or fragments of the shells of cockles, mussels or other shellfish.

The pellets also vary considerably in size. Some, belonging to a robin or wren are as small as a pea; others, such as those of a heron or seagull, may be as big as a golf ball or a sausage. They may be round or oval, thick or thin, neat or ragged.

There is still quite a lot we have to learn about bird pellets. We do not know exactly how they are formed, nor why some birds make them while others appear not to.

It is not difficult to find pellets; identifying them is a much bigger problem. The smaller birds such as robins, wagtails and dunnocks, for instance move about a lot when feeding, and they do not seem to eject their pellets at any particular period of the day. This is also true of species such as flycatchers, swifts and kingfishers, and most pellets are likely to be found beneath nests, unless you are lucky enough to see the bird actually produce a pellet while it is feeding.

A visit to a rookery or heronry in the breeding season can hardly go unrewarded. I have collected as many as 82 pellets beneath the trees where seven of the huge, untidy nests of herons were situated.

Many birds of prey have favourite spots where they perch to preen their feathers and, particularly in the morning, they often eject pellets while doing this. The perching place may be on a post supporting a wire fence, an old tree stump, an isolated tree, or a telegraph pole. Owl pellets are most likely to be found at nesting sites, although I have frequently come across them in open country.

As to identifying pellets, I can only give you a limited amount of guidance. The best evidence of identity is when you have seen a bird actually produce a pellet. Pellets that are found in, or under a nest you can assume have been made by the species of bird which resides there.

Small pellets, 1 cm long or less, which seem to be almost entirely composed of insect parts, are likely to be those of flycatchers. Oval pellets, about 2·5 cm long, with fur and insect remains in them, were probably made by a kestrel. Large oval or even rounded pellets found underneath a hollow tree are most likely to be a tawny owl's. Pellets similar to these, but found on the floor of a barn or a large outbuilding are almost certainly those of a barn owl.

Oval pellets, about 2·5 cm long, and made up of husks of grain, may sometimes be found scattered in cornfields, or beneath large trees in parks. These were made by rooks. The pellets of the carrion crow are longer, about 5 to 7·5 cm, and often sausage-shaped. They are untidy and of mixed materials, and are usually found in fields or near small clumps of trees.

Having collected some pellets, you will probably want to dissect them in order to discover what food the bird that produced the pellet has been eating. The pellets are by no means the nasty, smelly or messy things that you might expect, bearing in mind where they have come from. They are a bit damp when first produced, but they dry quickly and are then quite inoffensive. Nevertheless, do wash your hands thoroughly after handling the pellets or, better still, wear rubber gloves.

The first task is to soak the pellets in warm water for an hour or two. Then pour the water away, and

Fig. 1. Equipment needed for dissecting bird pellets

place the pellet on a piece of clean blotting paper.
Gently tease it out with a pair of forceps or two
mounted needles (old hat pins are useful).

Try to separate the various types of material in the
pellet into little heaps—the bones of animals into one
heap, the fur, feathers or vegetable matter into
another, the wing-cases and legs of insects into a third
and so on. Incidentally some pellets contain an incredible amount of animal remains. The late Maxwell
Knight, once took 533 bones from an owl's pellet.

When you have done this, you can go on to examine
the contents of the heaps more carefully, and this is
where a good hand lens is useful. Do not worry if you
cannot, at first, identify every bone or insect part.
This will come by experience, and a visit to an experienced naturalist or a museum will help greatly.
One job you can do is to put all the skulls together;
all the limb bones, ribs, shoulder bones and vertebrae

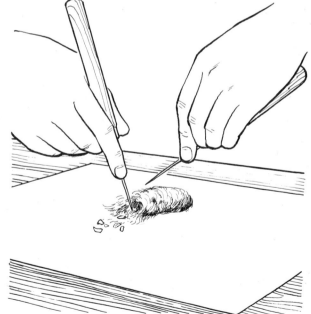

Fig. 2. Dissecting bird pellets

(the bones of the spine) in separate heaps. Bird skulls are easy to recognize, since the beaks usually remain attached. The skulls of mice, voles and other rodents can be identified by the large front teeth (incisors) adapted for gnawing; the skulls of shrews and moles can be recognized by the more even and sharp teeth necessary for chewing insects and worms.

If you want to make a permanent record of your work, then the material must be dried thoroughly. A piece of card of a suitable size will be necessary and on this you can stick with gum, first a whole pellet of the type you have been dissecting, next a specimen of the 'binding' material—the fur, feathers or vegetable matter, and finally a selection of the bones and insect parts that you have separated out. This done, write on the card the details about the pellet.

You can then go on to repeat this process with the pellets of other species until you have a representative collection.

OTHER COLLECTIONS OF FOOD REMAINS

A reference collection can also be made of the great variety of other food remains left behind by birds. Whenever you see birds feeding on natural foods, watch carefully until the birds have departed and then examine the spot where they were to see if they have left behind any clues as to what they were feeding on.

It is well worth-while keeping an eye on pine trees. Woodpeckers often wedge cones in the rough bark of a tree so that these can be hammered, to enable the bird to extract seeds. On the ground beneath a pine tree, you may come across a cone, the scales of which have been frayed; there is often a little piece of stem left at the base which looks as if it has been clipped with a pair of scissors—and this is not so far from the truth, for you are looking at the work of a crossbill. This bird, a species of finch, is very well adapted for dealing with cones. The beak in particular is most unusual; the upper half of it does not meet the lower half as in other birds, but is twisted so that it curves below the lower half. This allows the bird to 'scissor' the cone from the tree, leaving only the little piece of stem. Remember though, that other animals also eat cones. Mice and voles gnaw and nibble them and leave behind the evidence of their teeth, and squirrels remove all the scales with the exception of those at the tip of the cone.

Oak, hornbeam, hazel and beech trees are also well worth examining for evidence of feeding activities. Fragments of nutshells wedged in the bark of a tree are often the work of a nuthatch. Woodpeckers sometimes use a piece of bark as a vice, but their powerful beaks tend to destroy the nutshell completely. Numerous small nutshells or fruit stones are often found beneath trees and bushes; in cases where the shells have been neatly split in two, and have no teeth marks on them, we have clues to the presence of a hawfinch, which is the largest of our finches, and has a powerful beak quite capable of splitting a hard cherry or plum stone. The presence of that attractive winter visitor, the waxwing, can usually be detected by the skins of berries scattered on the ground beneath the bushes the birds have visited.

Fig. 3. A thrush's anvil

If you keep your eyes open, you will sooner or later come across a stone surrounded by pieces of snail shells. These stones are known as 'thrushes' anvils'. What happens is this: a thrush, on finding a snail, will pick up the snail by the rim of its shell, go to its favourite stone and hammer the shell until it breaks, thus revealing the juicy animal inside. Voles are fond of snails as well, but generally it is possible to see where the shells have been gnawed.

Completely empty shells which show no signs of damage at all are usually the work of glow worms.

These are just a few of the distinctive food remains that some birds leave behind. A collection of them can be of great value since they will be very useful to refer to when you find food remains but have not seen the bird responsible. A collection of the food leftovers of such mammals as mice, voles and squirrels will be useful for comparison.

PLASTER CASTS

Whilst out bird-watching one often comes across the impressions made by birds' feet on soft ground. Along the seashore and at the margins of lakes, ponds and streams prints are most common, but they can also be found in the fine soil of newly-raked seed beds or on the dusty surface of a path. If needs be, a small area of garden can be raked smooth and thoroughly wetted to ensure that tracks are left by visiting birds.

Perfect prints are very rare—a small leaf, a stone or a twig will all too often spoil the impression made by the bird's foot. If your aim is to collect only perfect prints, you will automatically tend to ignore all those which are imperfect. As a result you will lose much of the pleasure and interest that can be gained from a study of footprints. The making of casts should be a means to an end, and not an end in itself, and the study of footprints will lead eventually to a knowledge not only of the identity of the bird which made any particular set of tracks, but also of what it was doing at the time; whether it was drinking, preening, feeding, running from a predator or about to take flight.

What will you need for making plaster casts? The basic materials are few and quite inexpensive. A supply of Plaster of Paris, obtainable from chemists, ironmongers stores or builders merchants, should be kept in an air-tight tin, jar or plastic box. The powder should be fine in texture and fresh. Dental plaster gives the best results but is more expensive. You will also need some strips of thin card 3 to 5 cm wide and about 45 cm long, and a few paper clips. Some

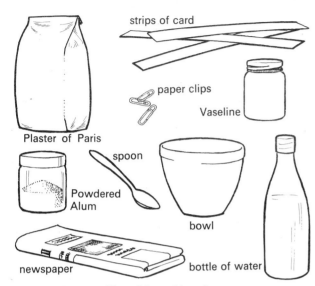

Fig. 4. What you will need for making plaster casts

just thick enough to run. There should be no air bubbles or lumps in the mixture.

Pour the liquid plaster slowly into the cardboard ring and smooth it over to produce a level surface. The plaster should be at least 2 cm thick. The cast can then be left to dry. This may take ten to fifteen minutes, or longer on a humid day, during which time you can write the necessary details in your notebook.

Soft sand is not suitable for taking good casts, and much care must be taken when pouring in your plaster. Do this as close to the footprint as you can— do not pour from a height or the plaster will spoil the impression.

vaseline and powdered alum will also be required, although you will not require much of either at any one time. The other items, which can be obtained quite easily, are some newspaper for wrapping up the casts to carry them home, a spoon, a plastic or enamel basin for mixing the paste, and a quantity of water in a plastic bottle.

Having selected your footprints, bend one of the card strips around in the shape of an oval or circle of sufficient size to enclose the whole of the footprint that you want. Paper-clip the overlapping ends and smear a little vaseline inside the ring to stop the plaster from sticking.

Pour some water into the basin and dissolve a pinch of alum in it. Now add the Plaster of Paris to the water, a little at a time. Work it in until you have a mixture which has the appearance and texture of cream, and is

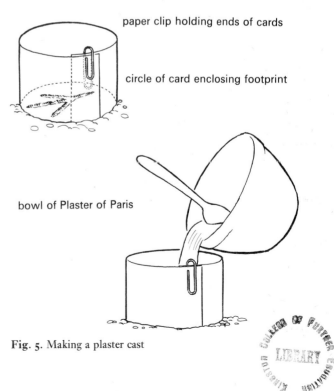

Fig. 5. Making a plaster cast

KINGSTON COLLEGE OF FURTHER EDUCATION LIBRARY

Snow also presents problems as the plaster mixture is warmer than the snow in which the track has been made, and as you pour the plaster the snow will melt. Until you are more experienced you must be content with sketches or photographs of tracks made in snow.

Having made your plaster cast, do not be in a hurry to see how it has come out. Loosely wrap the whole thing up in newspaper—plaster, card and soil, take it home and complete the work there; peel the cardboard away and using an old soft toothbrush gently wash and brush off any adhering mud particles.

You can, if you wish, paint the footprint so that it stands out from the rest of the cast. Use a dark colour for the actual footprint and a light colour for the surrounding plaster. Household emulsion paint or poster paint is best since plaster is fairly absorbent. On the back of the cast, the details of the bird that produced the print can be written in Indian ink, together with the place, and date upon which the cast was collected. When paint and ink are dry, the whole cast can be given a coat of clear varnish to enhance its appearance still further.

Fig. 6. A completed plaster cast

The completed casts may be stored in a drawer or neatly arranged on the shelves in a cabinet. If you wish to hang them up, a loop of tape must be included before you pour the last lot of plaster into the mould when making the cast.

Do not be downhearted if you have a few failures when you first start this fascinating study. We all make mistakes to begin with, but you should soon become skilled at making casts and before long you will go through all the stages almost automatically.

NESTS

When the fledglings have left a nest and it has fallen into disuse, you might like to take the nest to form a part of your bird museum.

Whenever possible you should try to take a nest complete with the branches or vegetation on which it rests. You must approach the owner of the land and get his permission before attempting to take even the smallest branch from one of his trees or bushes.

In the case of a fragile nest such as that of the long-tailed tit, it may be necessary to wind some brightly coloured thread many times round the nest in several directions to bind it to the branch, thereby ensuring that it does not disintegrate or become damaged while the sawing is in progress. The nest will be even further protected if someone holds the branch for you while you do the sawing, and the nest should remain bound with thread until it has been mounted.

More robust nests, such as those built by song thrushes and blackbirds, can sometimes be removed

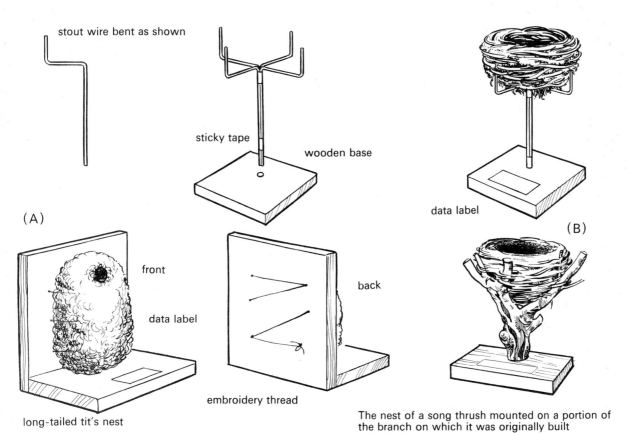

stout wire bent as shown

sticky tape

wooden base

data label

(A)

(B)

front

data label

back

embroidery thread

long-tailed tit's nest

The nest of a song thrush mounted on a portion of the branch on which it was originally built

Fig. 7. Wooden stands for birds' nest

temporarily from the branch while it is being cut, and then returned to their original position afterwards.

No special treatment is required before the nests are mounted, but if any of the specimens are damp they should be put near a radiator or on a sunny window ledge to dry. Mount the nests on labelled wooden stands of the kind shown in Figs. 7a and 7b. The type of nest will dictate the exact shape of mount you are to use.

SKELETONS

The skulls and skeletons of birds are extremely delicate objects and a study of them will teach you much about the way in which a bird is formed. In the course of your walks and your daily journeys to school, you are certain to find birds which have died, usually as a result of a motor accident. Their death will be slightly less of a tragedy if you learn something from the bodies of these birds. I would strongly emphasise the need to wear rubber gloves throughout the task of preparing your specimens, right up to the time when the bones have been bleached.

It is extremely difficult to make a complete skeleton and it is a good idea to start with the skulls of birds and then later, when you have gained experience, to try to mount a complete skeleton. It is best to begin with the head of a large bird and you could do no better than to ask the butcher to save the head of a chicken for you to practice the technique on.

You must begin by removing as much as possible of the skin, feathers and flesh from the bones, using a sharp knife or a scalpel. The fleshing process will include removal of the brain, and this is best done by inserting a hooked wire into the large rounded opening at the base of the skull. The wire is then twisted and turned so that the brain breaks up and may be removed piece by piece.

When the fleshing is complete there follows a process of *maceration*, which is always accompanied by a rather horrid odour, and should be carried out in a shed or garage away from the house, or in a school laboratory where there is a fume-cupboard.

To macerate the skull, place it in a jar and cover it with water. The jar itself must then be covered with a piece of cloth to prevent the entry of dust and flies. Within a week or so the flesh which remains will have reached a sufficiently advanced stage of decomposition for the specimen to be subjected to the next stage of

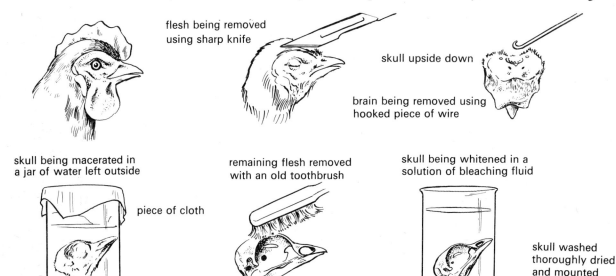

flesh being removed using sharp knife

skull upside down

brain being removed using hooked piece of wire

skull being macerated in a jar of water left outside

piece of cloth

remaining flesh removed with an old toothbrush

skull being whitened in a solution of bleaching fluid

skull washed thoroughly dried and mounted

Note: All operations carried out wearing rubber gloves.

Fig. 8. Preparing a chicken's skull

treatment. This involves removing it from the macerating jar and carefully brushing it, under running water, with an old toothbrush, to rid it of the decomposed flesh. In addition to brushing, you may find it necessary to pick your way around the various cavities with a mounted needle (or an old hat-pin) in order to loosen odd pieces of flesh which cannot be reached with the brush. This should be done whilst the skull is held under running water.

If all has gone according to plan, the skull should now be entirely free of flesh. Nevertheless in its present state it looks very much discoloured. It can be whitened by submerging it for an hour or two in a solution of one of the household bleaching fluids. Keep a regular check on the skull because when it is sufficiently bleached, it must be removed, otherwise the chemical will harm it.

After removal of the skull from the bleaching fluid, rinse it in running water, dry it as much as possible with a soft absorbent cloth, and leave it exposed to the warm air of a room to become dry throughout.

The skull may then be attached to a square of thick card or thin plywood with polystyrene cement, labelled, and stored in a glass-topped box or one of transparent plastic.

If this has seemed a grisly section do not forget that all creatures must die eventually, and there is a great deal to be learned from observing and investigating them after death. As long as you are careful in handling them, and thoroughly wash your hands afterwards with soap and water, you will come to no harm. Skulls and other bones are particularly well worth preserving and studying, because from them you will learn much about how birds are made and fitted for their particular way of life.

FEATHERS AND WINGS

Feathers, wherever they have come from, are of two main kinds: outer flight or contour feathers which give the bird its shape and stop the body from losing heat, and inner down feathers which provide an extra warm layer like a vest. Other types of feathers have features of both these basic kinds, or have developed from them.

The typical flight or contour feather is made up of a central shaft, hollow at its base for absorbing food materials, and becoming solid for strength further up, in a part called the *rhachis*, where the two webs of the *vane* are supported (Fig. 10a). These webs are marvellously intricate structures. They consist of hundreds of parallel barbs, each almost a complete feather in itself, for every barb in turn carries several

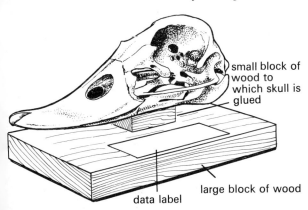

small block of wood to which skull is glued

large block of wood

data label

Fig. 9. A mounted mallard's skull

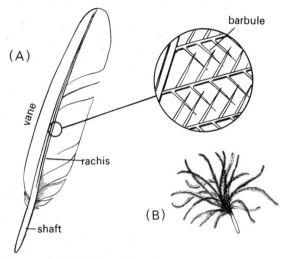

Fig. 10. Typical flight and down feathers

hundred tiny barbules, equipped with minute hooks. The hooks catch on the barbules from the next barb above them. This fastening system is so efficient that if two barbs are separated and the web is split, the bird merely has to draw the feather through its beak a few times to restore the web to its proper shape. You can straighten up a ruffled feather by running it between your finger and thumb.

Down feathers are fluffy because their barbules have no hooks. (Fig. 10b.)

When a bird fluffs itself out in cold weather, it is giving itself a thicker blanket of warm air between its inner and outer covering of feathers. In warm weather the bird often disarranges its outer feathers to speed up the process of heat loss. Birds need good insulation, especially against cold, because they live at what for us would be fever heat; they must maintain a body temperature of about 41°C. In very severe winters,

when food is scarce, even feathers cannot always prevent birds from freezing to death.

Birds are the most vividly coloured of all backboned creatures, though by no means all of them are brightly coloured. As a general rule, the warmer and drier the climate, the brighter the bird. British birds tend to be more drably coloured than those which live in the Tropics. The colours of birds have two opposite functions, for one is to enable the bird to advertise its presence and the other is to conceal it. In many species a balance is struck between these two needs; the male is brightly coloured, especially in the breeding season, and the female is camouflaged by drab colours so that she is hidden from the eyes of enemies while sitting on her nest. The bright plumage of such birds as the cock pheasant does more than simply attract a mate; it serves too as a kind of battle flag to warn off rivals when the bird is defending its territory.

Keep all the good clean feathers you find or are given, and mount them on a sheet of paper or card using sticky tape. If you find a dead bird, some of the more interesting or important feathers can be cut off from it. You could also remove a wing from the corpse and mount this, since it will teach you a lot about the way these limbs are made up.

In late summer and early autumn odd feathers are to be found in secluded spots—under bushes or in thickets. They are usually feathers from a bird which is moulting, for the plumage is not shed wholesale, but little by little. Feathers which have been moulted are easily recognised. They look worn and the colours are dull. The end of the shaft is dry and may even be cracked. Feathers from a bird in full plumage on the other hand, are sleek and bright. Add examples of both kinds to your collection for comparison.

Remember when you mount your specimens that sticky tapes such as Sellotape stick to anything they touch, and you must be extremely careful when sticking single feathers or whole wings not to ruin your specimen by destroying the texture of the feathers. An alternative to the use of Sellotape is to mount your specimens of feathers and wings between two sheets of the sticky transparent plastic that can be obtained in small pieces from your local stationers. This material is sold under a variety of trade names including Transpaseal, Fablon and Contact. When this technique is used the specimens are preserved intact and cannot be damaged by dust, insects or other nuisances, but again care is necessary not to allow the sticky material to destroy the texture of the feathers.

white paper or card

label

sellotape

sellotape

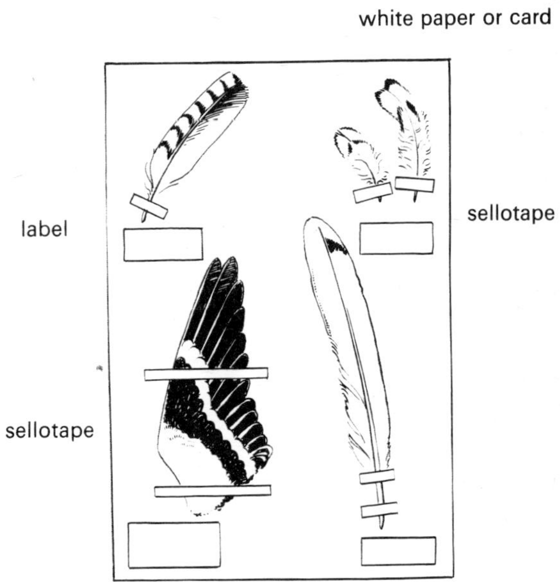

Fig. 11. Mounting feathers and wings

CHAPTER FIVE

Some Easy Projects

This chapter contains some ideas for simple projects which will give you the chance to discover new facts for yourself about bird life and bird behaviour. None of these projects is particularly difficult; with care you should be able to carry out most or all of them if you have the time and patience.

Perhaps a word of advice about what is sometimes called the *Scientific Method* would not be out of place here. This may sound deadly dull and boring, but it need not be. Scientific bird-watching is simply bird-watching in which you make sure about everything that you observe, and try and answer the questions that spring to mind. At some time or another, most bird-watching beginners have prepared to put down in their notes 'Saw a golden oriole', only to discover on closer investigation that they had seen in fact, the much less rare green woodpecker flying in the sun-light between the trees.

Before you start your first project or experiment, therefore, let us consider what you have to do to get accurate or scientific results.

Always state your problem clearly so that you know exactly what you are hoping to find out. Plan carefully, get good advice, and learn any facts and techniques that will be useful for the project. If possible work with someone who shares your interests. Two heads are always better than one!

One of the best ways to make certain that everything is correct is to repeat the experiment or project many times to see if you always obtain the same kind of result. Test your results in every way. Think of possible causes of error. Invite your friends to criticise your results, and see if you get the same answer when you attack the problem in an entirely different way.

Always gather as much evidence as you can before you draw your final conclusions. It is unscientific to be satisfied with only one experiment. Keep asking yourself 'Why?'. Why does the bird stop to preen itself in the middle of a fight with another bird? Why does it attack the wheel-hub of a car? Why does it do this? Why does it do that? If you try and find the answers to your questions you will soon find that one project or experiment will lead you on to a whole range of others, and you will have embarked upon the exciting path of scientific research.

Finally, never lose sight of the fact that the bird is your real object of study and should always come first. If you ever feel your experiments are causing disturbance to the bird or are likely to endanger it in any way, *Stop!* No experiment which causes death or cruelty to a living creature is worth continuing. Birds have enough natural enemies to contend with, without your adding to the list.

FEEDING TIMES

Do birds eat continuously throughout the day if given the chance, or do they have definite meal times?

Before any observations can be carried out on this subject, it is essential that the birds should be used to finding food whenever they come to the bird table and not just at a few separate periods, say after you have had your breakfast or lunch. It is therefore necessary to keep the bird table well supplied with breadcrumbs or some other food, each day from dawn until dusk, for at least a week before you carry out your observations. Then you can record the number of birds of each species seen feeding at the bird table for a fifteen minute period during each hour of the day.

You might set out your results something like this:

Date: 14th December 1976

Time   Species   Observations
7:00 a.m.   1 Robin   Flew away with bread which it ate on fence.

8:00am –   9 Starlings } All ate
8:15 am   3 House   } greedily
            Sparrows

and so on, preferably until dusk.

A brief note on the weather conditions during the day would also be useful. Repeat this type of observation at different seasons of the year.

If birds do have definite meal times, do they vary from day to day, and does the weather make any difference? Do different species have their meals at different times?

Coffee jar lids nailed to plank of wood, each lid contains a different kind of seed.

Fig. 1. An experiment on seed-eating

SEED-EATING

During the summer and autumn, make a collection of as many different kinds of seeds as possible from the garden, hedgerows, fields, waste ground, and so on. Allow the seeds to dry in the sun and then keep them in labelled packets until they are needed. If you wish you can buy a selection of seeds from a corn merchant.

Fasten a series of equal-sized small containers, such as coffee jar lids or match box trays, to the bird table or a plank of wood on the ground. Spread out the containers so that the birds have enough elbow room when feeding (Fig. 1).

For a few days in winter put out a little seed mixture (a home-made one, or one from a shop such as 'Swoop') into each of the containers so that the birds get used to feeding from all of them. Then begin the experiment proper by putting small but exactly equal amounts of the seeds you have collected into the containers—a different kind of seed in each container. Repeat the experiment over several days, varying the containers used for any particular type of seed.

From your observations, you will discover which species eat which kinds of seeds, and which seeds are the most popular.

One of the advantages of this type of experiment is that if it is carried out over a long period it will tell you the kind of food to put out on your bird table to attract any particular species of bird.

PLATE VII. A Green Woodpecker   **PLATE VIII.** Great Spotted Woodpecker

INVERTEBRATE FOOD PREFERENCES OF BIRDS

The study of the invertebrate food preferences of birds is more difficult than that of other foods, mainly because of the problem of preventing the small invertebrates from escaping.

Each box is covered with strips of thin transparent polythene or cellophane.

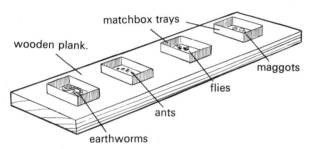

Fig. 2. Using the trays of matchboxes to show the invertebrate food preferences of birds

The simplest piece of apparatus to use is a series of small cardboard boxes; the trays of matchboxes will do. Fasten these at intervals along a plank of wood using drawing pins (Fig. 2). A number of strips of thin transparent cellophane or polythene will also be needed, together with a reel of Sellotape.

Put a few live earthworms in one box and tightly sellotape the cellophane or polythene over the top so that the worms cannot escape. In the next box put woodlice, in the next earwigs, in the next ants, flies or maggots, or whatever is available, and so on.

Place the board in a conspicuous place on the lawn and keep watch. It may be necessary to attract the birds with a few bread crumbs. As soon as a bird comes along, watch carefully and see if it attempts to take any of the invertebrates from the boxes. If it does, record which box is attacked and then repair the box and start again. Gradually, by this procedure, you will learn which invertebrate foods a whole range of species prefer out of the types that you offer them.

BIRDS AND WASPS

A number of birds including song thrushes and spotted flycatchers will eat wasps in late summer, when wasps are in abundance. Obtain a number of ripe fallen apples, crush them in a shallow dish so as to release the juice, and leave them in the open where wasps can find them. Watch carefully, and make a list of the birds which come after the wasps. Have the birds any way of getting rid of the sting? How do they approach a wasp so as to avoid being stung?

SONG THRUSHES AND SNAILS

(a) Collect and examine the snail shells broken open by song thrushes, also watch the birds actually breaking the shells. Is the same method of holding and cracking the shells used every time?

(b) Collect as many species of the common garden snail as you can. Paint the shells of half the snails with a quick-drying enamel paint in a bright colour. Put

Fig. 3. Song thrushes and snails

all the snails on a lawn or in some other conspicuous spot, and observe which of the snails are removed by song thrushes. Try different colours such as red, yellow, blue, white, and so on, in combination with examples of the natural coloured snails, and find out the colours that song thrushes take most of. Do the thrushes like certain colours best, or are these the ones that they can see most easily?

(c) Song thrushes often take empty snail shells to their 'anvils', as their favourite stones are called, and leave them unbroken. It would seem that it never occurs to the thrush that the shell it is carrying is lighter than ones in which it has previously found food. Pack empty snail shells with differing amounts of clay or plasticine and leave the shells in a prominent position; on a lawn or concrete path. How do the thrushes react to these artificial snails? If a snail shell is too heavy for the thrush to carry, what does it do?

FEEDING ON BERRIES

During the autumn and winter keep a watch on those trees and shrubs that bear berries, to see which species of birds eat berries and which kinds they prefer. Record your observations in the form of a table listing the date, place, number and species of birds, and the type of berries they were eating. A brief note on the weather conditions when each record was made would also be useful. Remember that you should only record details of those birds actually *seen eating* the berries, and not just those that were sitting in the tree or bush where the berries were.

GREAT TITS AND HAZEL NUTS

Great tits, grey squirrels, mice and a number of other animals eat hazel nuts in winter and drop the empty shells close to their feeding places.

Put some hazel nuts on the bird table, wait until the nuts have been opened by great tits, and then collect the empty shells as specimens. Towards the end of winter, if there is a hazel tree near your home, collect as many of the opened hazel nut shells as you can from the leaf litter under and around the tree. What proportion of them have been opened by great tits? Try and identify the animals responsible for opening the other shells. Repeat these observations in as many different areas as possible and over a number of years. Does the proportion of hazel nuts eaten by great tits vary from place to place, and from year to year in the same place?

KESTRELS' FEEDING ACTIVITIES

The kestrel is still quite common in most parts of Britain, in spite of the large scale use of poisonous chemicals designed to kill some of the creatures on which it preys. If you live in London your chances of seeing a kestrel are just as good as they would be if you lived in the country, since the bird is to be found in some of the parks and in the outer open spaces such as Richmond Park and Hampstead Heath.

When looking for food the kestrel usually hovers, with wings fluttering, far above the ground. If it sees nothing of interest it flies on a little way and hovers again. If, however, the movement of some suitable object of prey, such as a field vole, catches its eye, the kestrel will drop lower, hover again, and then when it thinks it has a chance of seizing the quarry, it will suddenly swoop to the ground. If it has been lucky, it will soon rise up into view with the vole held in its talons, and fly off to a tree, building or some other vantage point to eat it; if as often happens, the prey has escaped, the kestrel will continue its hovering and searching.

What proportion of the kestrel's dives to the ground are successful? It is helpful to express your results as a percentage, worked out in the following way:

$$\frac{number\ of\ successful\ dives}{total\ number\ of\ dives\ (successful\ plus\ unsuccessful)} \times 100$$

Compare the percentages obtained in different localities and in different months of the year. What is the kestrel's food throughout the year? Collect pellets (see page 56), to discover this.

FEEDING ACTIVITIES OF SPOTTED FLYCATCHERS

PLATE IX. A Willow Warbler

Most birds, if they eat insects at all, will sometimes try to catch insects in flight. The spotted flycatcher feeds mainly on insects that it has caught on the wing; the bird remains on its perch for several seconds at a time, then darts into the air to snatch an insect, returning as a rule to the same perch.

Fig. 4. Spotted flycatcher catching insects

Observing the feeding activities of a flycatcher is quite easy since the bird almost always chooses the same perch from which to hawk insects. Watch the bird carefully and note how often it is successful in catching insects (use binoculars for this). Record your results as a percentage, worked out as follows:

$$\frac{number\ of\ flights\ when\ insects\ were\ caught}{number\ of\ attempts\ (successful\ and\ unsuccessful)} \times 100$$

How do the percentages vary under different weather conditions?

In the late summer if you see a young flycatcher, which can be recognised by its lighter plumage with inconspicuous dark spots on the breast, compare its percentage success at catching insects with that of adult birds that have had much more experience at hawking for food. Are young flycatchers born with the ability to catch insects fully developed, or does the ability improve with practise?

FOOD STORAGE

Most birds have no thought for the future where food is concerned. There are however, a few species that instinctively lay up stores of food for use later on. Amongst those that are likely to visit your garden are the nuthatch, coal and marsh tits, and most members of the crow family. Usually they bury each seed, nut or piece of bread singly in the ground, or push it into a crevice in the bark of a branch or tree-trunk, and carefully cover it up before leaving. Nuthatches in particular will carry away peanut after peanut or lump after lump of bread until nothing is left.

There is still a great deal to be found out about the food storing habits of birds and all examples of storing should be carefully recorded. Note particularly the species of bird involved, the type of food, and exactly where and how it was hidden. Do any of the birds that you have watched hiding food, find it again? If so, do you think that the bird remembered exactly where the food was hidden, or did it merely find the food again by chance through searching in likely places?

FEEDING LEVELS OF BIRDS

Birds can be broadly divided into three groups according to where they feed. Ground feeders such as the dunnock, robin, pheasant and partridge, feed mainly on the ground. Tree feeders such as blue tits, great tits, tree-creepers and woodpeckers largely confine their feeding activities to trees and bushes, while aerial feeders such as the swallow, swift and martin feed while actually in flight.

Of course this is only a rough and ready classification. You may well see a green woodpecker on the ground attacking an ants' nest, or a dunnock searching the branches of a tree for insects concealed in the bark. Some birds are difficult to put in any one particular category. However, these three groups do provide a good basis for study, particularly if surveys are carried out on them throughout the year so that comparisons can be drawn.

Make lists of the birds that come in each of these three groups and then try and find out which type of ground each of the species of ground feeders prefers, e.g. lawn, long grass, paths, freshly dug ground, undergrowth, etc. What type of food is being collected? Does the ground preference change from one season to another? If so why?

In the case of tree feeders, which type of trees or shrubs are preferred by each species. Does the preference change from season to season, if so why? Record the height above ground that you see each of the species feeding. Compare the averages for a large number of sightings for each species. You might for example find that during the month of June, you saw no blue tits feeding on the ground, only a few feeding above 11 metres, with the vast majority feeding at a height of between 2 and 11 metres, with the average at 5 metres. You could then compare these results with those you obtained for great tits and other tree feeders.

In the case of aerial feeders, study is much more difficult. You might, however, try and estimate the

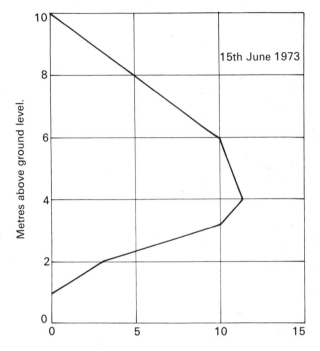

Fig. 5. Feeding levels of garden blue tits

height at which these birds are hawking for insects and see whether the feeding height varies according to the weather conditions.

DRINKING

All birds require water, although different species drink different amounts. This is because some water is obtained from the food and in all probability the more succulent the food is the less water the bird will have to drink.

Make a list of all the species that you observe drinking from the garden pool or bird bath, and make notes on how they drink. Also try and record how often each species drinks and try and relate this to their food. For example, do seed-eating birds drink more or less than insect-eaters?

BIRDS ATTACKING MILK BOTTLES

The habit of certain species of birds of attacking milk bottle tops, and in some cases drinking the cream, seems to be spreading to more and more species. In a survey carried out during 1967-68 by members of the Young Ornithologists' Club it was revealed that as many as 20 species of wild birds have been observed to attack milk bottles, and reports were received from practically every county in the British Isles.

You cannot hope to repeat such a large-scale survey on your own, but you can carry out a survey amongst your friends and neighbours, preferably monthly over a whole year. The local milkmen will probably be able to give you information as well.

During which months are most attacks reported? Do the birds show preference for any particular coloured tops, if so is it the one with most cream? Are the bottles and cartons of fresh cream and yoghurt that some milkmen deliver ever attacked? Do the birds ever touch the milk bottles while they are still on the milkman's float or at the dairy? Are the milk bottles in some parts of your town or village more prone to attack than others? If so, can you find out why? What sort of precautions do people take to stop their milk being taken by the birds?

SEASONAL VARIATION IN THE BIRD SPECIES PRESENT IN A GARDEN

List all the bird species seen in the garden every week or every month for a whole year. Record your results on a simple chart, like the one shown below, which will reveal the species that are resident and those that are summer or winter visitors. Use reference books to help you to find out where the migrant species travel to or have come from.

The chart set out below shows the presence or absence of just three species during each month of the year.

Month:

	Jan.	Feb.	Mar.	Apr.	May	June	July	Aug.	Sept.	Oct.	Nov.	Dec.
Robin	×	×	×	×	×	×	×	×	×	×	×	×
Song thrush	×	×	×	×	×	×	×	×	×	×	×	×
House martin	—	—	—	×	×	×	×	×	×	×	—	—

Keep a careful record of the dates of the arrival and departure of migrant bird species and compare these with the records for other years. Are the dates of arrival or departure connected with the type of weather? For example, do the swallows or martins leave Britain earlier during a cold or wet autumn than they do if the weather is mild and sunny?

A CENSUS OF BIRDS

There are various ways of carrying out a census to estimate the bird population of an area. You could, for example, confine yourself to a large garden or a park or playing field and take regular counts, preferably weekly, of the numbers of each species that you see within that area. Alternatively, you could concentrate on the numbers of a few selected species such as blackbirds, starlings and chaffinches. The counting is best done in the early morning when most birds are to be seen and when many are singing. Quietness is essential if you are not to drive all the birds away. After several counts you should be able to assess your results and obtain a fair estimate of the numbers of each species within your chosen area. This result can then be compared with those for other seasons of the year.

Another method of carrying out a census is less accurate but much quicker and easier. It consists of a walk through a piece of country, counting the birds on the way. You could do it on your way to school each morning, even if you travel by bus, or when you are exercising a dog or on a favourite walk. Your totals

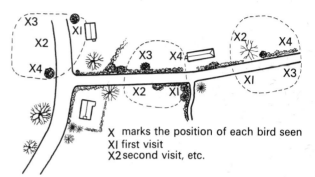

X marks the position of each bird seen
X1 first visit
X2 second visit, etc.

After several visits you will notice that the crosses occur in little groups on your map. Each little cluster of crosses represents a territory occupied by one breeding pair of their species.

Fig. 6. A census of dunnocks in a country lane

for the week or month can then be added up and compared with those for other weeks or months. This type of census will not tell you the total number of birds in the area you have walked, but it will indicate seasonal variations in their numbers, and such features as migration patterns.

GULL FLOCKS

Even in big towns it is a common sight to see large flocks of gulls on school playing fields, football and cricket pitches, and in similar areas. Keep records of the visits of all these flocks. Is the flock made up of just one kind of gull, or several kinds? Are the birds adult or immature? What are they feeding on? Do the numbers in the flocks vary according to the weather or to the time of day or time of year?

GULL CALL NOTES

Put out quite large quantities of bread crumbs in an area where gulls are likely to be around. When a gull has seen the food supply, listen carefully for the call notes it makes. Try to write them down. Do all gulls of the species make this particular type of call to inform their fellows of the presence of food? Repeat the experiment on another day but only put out one or two pieces of bread. Does the first gull to arrive still make the same call? Can you see any instances where gulls share the food they have found with others of their own kind?

BIRD SONG

There is a tremendous variation in the amount that birds sing, not only from season to season but also during the course of any particular day. It is, therefore, instructive to note those days on which you hear a few selected species sing, and to make a chart to record the distribution of their song throughout the year.

Put a tick or a cross if you hear any of these species singing during each month.

Then, on one day each month, record the hours that each of these species is singing. If you are able to keep a record of the weather conditions such as temperature, cloud cover, air pressure, and wind strength, your results will be even more valuable since you may be able to find out whether the output of song is affected by the various changes in the weather.

DAWN CHORUS

A study of the dawn chorus requires a great ability to recognise bird song, and to begin with, it is suggested that you choose to study only two or three species whose songs you can easily recognize.

The object of the exercise is to discover which birds sing first each day. It is a matter of getting up before dawn on a spring morning and noting the order in which the birds begin to sing, the time when they begin to sing, and also the time at which the general chorus begins. The project will be of greater value if you repeat your observations several times and calculate the average of your results so that any variations due to differing weather conditions are eliminated.

	Jan.	Feb.	Mar.	Apr.	May	June	July	Aug.	Sept.	Oct.	Nov.	Dec.
Robin												
Blackbird												
Song thrush												
Wren												
Dunnock												

SONG-POSTS

Many birds have a favourite spot from which they sing, such as a prominent bough of a tree, a clothes post, chimney pot, television aerial, telegraph pole or lamp-post.

Map the song-posts of the birds in your garden, or in a small wood or park near your home. Do different species have a preference for certain types of song-post? Do song thrushes prefer television aerials? Do starlings prefer chimney pots? What is the preferred height of the song-posts of each species? There are several ways of measuring the height of tall objects. One of the simplest is to stand at a distance from the object to be measured, and estimate how many times larger it is than an object or person whose height you know. (Fig. 7). Is there any evidence that the number of suitable song-posts influences the number and distribution of birds in your area?

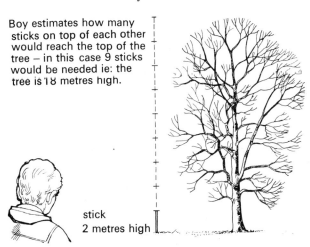

Boy estimates how many sticks on top of each other would reach the top of the tree – in this case 9 sticks would be needed ie: the tree is 18 metres high.

stick 2 metres high

Fig. 7. Measuring the height of a tall object

TERRITORY

Many birds occupy a 'territory', particularly during the breeding season. This is an area which they claim and defend, and on which the males sing to attract a mate and ward off rivals. It is possible to map a bird's territory if you begin patient and careful observations in the early spring when birds are just taking up residence (Fig. 8), Robins behave in an unusual way, in that they occupy a territory, although not always the same one, throughout the year.

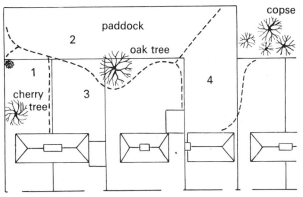

Fig. 8. The territories of four robins

Begin by drawing a sketch map of your own and neighbouring gardens, or if you have no garden, of the local park. Mark on it the spots where a particular bird is regularly to be seen singing. Robins, blackbirds, song thrushes, great tits and chaffinches have a strong territorial instinct and it is a good idea to begin with one of these species. Mark on the map the points where other birds are driven off. Note down the birds against which your chosen individual reacts, and those it ignores. Note the bird's behaviour during the day, and how the male reacts to the females. Gradually a clear picture of the extent of the bird's territory will emerge and other aspects of its fighting and courtship behaviour may be observed as well. Repeat this type of study with other common species.

Stuffed birds can also be used to discover the extent of a territory—see page 87.

BIRDS' NESTS

A very instructive study can be made of birds' nests. Some preliminary work can be done in the spring and summer, recording the position of any nests that you find and identifying the species to which they belong. A detailed study can begin in the autumn after the young birds have flown and the nest has been deserted.

Before you remove each nest, record its exact position including, if it is in a tree, the species of the tree

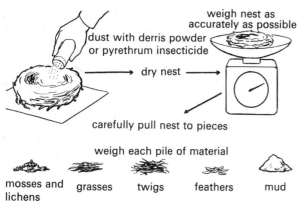

Fig. 9. Dissecting a bird's nest

and the height of the nest above ground. When you have removed the nest, it is a good plan to dust it with derris powder or one of the insect powders containing pyrethrum, to kill any parasites that may be lurking there, and then allow the nest to dry out thoroughly. Weigh the nest as accurately as you can and then carefully pull it to pieces. Separate the material into heaps—moss and lichens in one pile, dried grass in another, mud in another, twigs in another, and so on. Weigh or measure the contents of each pile.

Repeat this for as many nests as you can, and then draw up a list of the favourite nesting materials and favourite nest sites for each of the species you have studied.

A SURVEY OF HOUSE MARTINS' NESTS

Make a survey of house martins' nests in your area. If you have a large scale map (these can often be obtained free from an estate agent's office), you could mark in the approximate positions of the nests on the map.

There seem to be at least two kinds of house martins' nest: the common type which is constructed of mud and built under the eaves of a house or some other building, and a less common type which is similar in appearance to the first mentioned, but which is built into the corner of a window (Fig. 10). How many of each can you find?

Which aspect do the house martins prefer? Use a compass to find out if the nest is facing north, south,

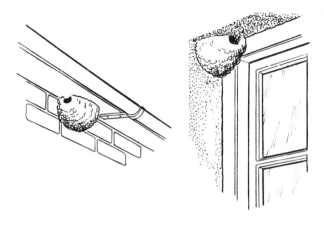

Fig. 10. Two kinds of house martins' nests

east or west. Do the birds seem to show any preference for any particular coloured paintwork when building nests under the eaves of houses. Are there more nests on old buildings than on new ones? Where do the martins obtain their supplies of mud? How many of the nests are subsequently taken over by house sparrows? How many nests are knocked down by the owners of the houses? You will probably find the reason given for doing this is that the birds foul the path or step with their droppings. This problem can be overcome quite easily by fitting a shelf just below the nest until the young birds have flown.

ROOSTING

Some birds such as rooks and carrion crows, which usually roost high in the bare branches of tall trees, do not seem to worry about shelter when roosting.

Most species, however, appear to seek some protection from wind and rain. The winter roosts of sparrows and finches are usually in thick evergreen trees and shrubs, and those of wagtails in thick bushes, bramble patches or dead reeds. If you watch starlings and pigeons roosting on buildings in towns, you will notice how they prefer those ledges best protected from wind and rain. In all these cases, however, it is possible that safety from predators is as important a factor as comfort.

Some species, notably starlings, rooks, crows, jackdaws, gulls, many finches, blackbirds, and thrushes, use large communal roosts in autumn and winter. Sometimes several species roost together. Other birds roosting together may be all of the same species; there is no hard and fast rule. You may see huge flocks of starlings that have arrived in this country from northern Europe flying to a communal roost, whilst other starlings are roosting at the same time singly or in pairs in ivy, on or near a house or on the rafters of an old barn or outbuilding.

Communal roosts of birds can be discovered by a simple piece of detective work. All you need to do is obtain a large scale map of the district and mark on it a long line showing the direction of flight of the first flocks of birds going to roost. Next evening go to a spot about a mile away, to the north or south of the spot where you saw the first flocks, and try to locate another batch of birds going to roost. Mark their direction of flight on the map. Repeat the process on several evenings until you have recorded a number of 'flight-lines' on your map. At the point where these lines cross, you should find the roost. Of course there may be more than one roost in the district and this will make your detective work harder but much more interesting.

Having found a roost, there is much more research that can be done. Measure the area covered and get there early to try and estimate the size of the flock. Keep records of the times of arrival of the birds and see how their arrival times are influenced by the length of the day and the weather conditions. Where do the birds go in the daytime? Do they remain in quite large flocks or do they break up into small groups to feed?

When you turn to those species which roost singly or in small groups, a different technique may have to be employed, which involves quietly searching likely spots with a dimmed torch.

Remember however, that a bird forced to leave its nest at night is in danger of being caught by an owl or of injuring itself as it flies in the dark. Another danger is that the bird may be unable to find a sheltered spot and be forced to sleep in some exposed place; this could mean death to an underfed small bird in winter. If, therefore, you feel you want to look for roosting birds, it is much kinder to go just before dawn when, if disturbed, the birds will have only a little time to wait until daylight.

Find out all you can about the type of situation each species uses for roosting; whether the bird usually roosts alone or in company, what times it goes to roost under a variety of weather conditions and if its roosting time changes throughout the year.

A more detailed study of the roosting habits of the tree-creeper is given in the next section.

ROOSTING HABITS OF THE TREE-CREEPER

When one considers that most of the world's 9,000 species of birds build nests, it is surprising that so few species build winter-nests for roosting. Some do, but these are not many. At least three of the European species of woodpecker chisel out a winter roost as well as a spring nursery. However, so far as is known, only one species in the world makes a roosting site using a technique different from the one it employs in nest building: the tree-creeper.

Fig. 11. A Wellingtonia or redwood tree

Until about 60 years ago the tree-creeper regularly used ready-made crevices for both breeding and sleeping.

In 1853, the Wellingtonia, or redwood tree was introduced to this country from North America. This tree has a very soft fibrous bark and by the turn of the century the first specimens had grown sufficiently for the spongy bark to be about 5 cm thick. In 1905 a remarkable discovery was made: a neat, rounded hole in the bark of a Wellingtonia in Scotland. It was at first thought to be the work of a woodpecker, but inspection with a lamp at night revealed a tree-creeper sleeping soundly in the cavity. Without any previous experience of excavation, the bird had made a do-it-yourself bed. Nowadays tree-creepers all over Britain are hacking out their own night-time roosts in Wellingtonia trees.

Fig. 12. A roosting tree-creeper

If there is one of these large conifers in your local park or in a cemetery, churchyard or garden, it is well worthwhile examining it carefully to see if it is used for roosting by tree-creepers. Such roosts are usually spotted easily since they are almost always marked by a white streak of droppings. Record the number of roosts in each tree and the height they are above the ground. So far as is known the tree-creeper always roosts alone, but a closely related species, the short-toed tree-creeper, which is common in Europe, roosts in company in very cold weather. Can you find any evidence that British tree-creepers roost together in a cold spell? Where do the local tree-creepers roost if there are no Wellingtonias in the neighbourhood? What time do they go to bed and at what time do they rise throughout the year? Please remember, however, the precautions mentioned in the previous section about the dangers of disturbing roosting birds.

DOMINANCE

When watching birds in your garden or in a park, you will probably have noticed that many birds which normally find their own food will turn to robbery if they get the chance. For example, a mistle thrush will often try to force the smaller song thrush to drop the worm it has found. Sometimes the food may change hands—or rather bills, several times before it is finally swallowed. Keep records of all cases of this type of robbery and gradually build up a list showing the dominance of the various species. At the bottom of the list will be the species that regularly loses the food it has found but which on the other hand never succeeds in robbing another bird. At the top of your list will be the bully that is always stealing food from another species but is never itself robbed.

REACTIONS OF BIRDS TO MODELS OF PREDATORS

Fit a length of wire between two trees or between two clothes posts, above a lawn where birds normally feed. By means of pieces of bent wire, attach a model hawk, quite a crude model will do, to the wire so that, by the device shown in Fig. 13, it can be moved backwards and forwards along the wire.

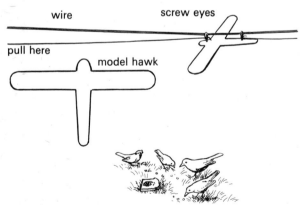

Fig. 13. A model hawk

When birds are feeding on the lawn below, slowly pull the model along the wire, first in a forwards direction and later backwards. Note how the birds react in each case. Later try pulling the model across

quickly. You may go on to experiment with other shapes, including those shown in Fig. 14, and note what any effects they have, on the small birds.

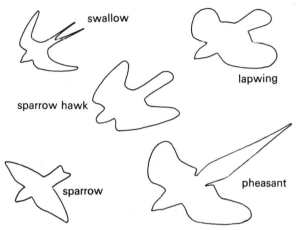

Fig. 14. Some other model birds

Similarly, try and find out how birds recognize owls. Begin by cutting out a large copy of the shape shown in Fig. 15 in stout card, hardboard or plywood. Set it in a prominent position in the garden and watch carefully to see how the birds react. Remove the model, draw a large pair of eyes on it and replace it a few hours later to see how the birds behave towards it. Still later on add the beak, then an outline of the wings, the talons, details of the feathers, and the correct colouring.

When you have discovered by which feature or features birds recognize owls and hawks, you might if you are able, repeat these experiments above a pen containing the young of the domesticated chicken, duck or goose and see how they react. Are young birds born with the ability to recognize their enemies? In

Fig. 15. A model owl

other words is this an instinct, or is it something which they have to learn from their parents or by experience?

Please remember that experiments on the reactions of wild birds to model predators should not be carried out during the nesting season when parent birds may be distressed sufficiently to desert their eggs or young.

REACTIONS OF BIRDS TO STUFFED PREDATORS

If you are able to obtain a stuffed owl, hawk, fox, weasel, stoat or some other creature that preys on birds, set it up in a lifelike position on the lawn if it is a mammal, or on a prominent branch if it is a bird, and observe carefully the reactions of the garden birds.

Which species are alarmed by the predator? Do they react by giving an alarm call or do they actually try to attack or mob the stuffed creature? What happens when the predator will not go away?

Fig. 16. Using a stuffed fox to test the reactions of birds to predators

Similar studies can be carried out with stuffed passerine or perching birds such as robins, blackbirds, great tits and the like, during the early spring to see how the resident birds react to the intruder. In fact a stuffed bird can be useful in helping to find the limits of a bird's territory since, if you move it around you will be able to see exactly where in the garden it is attacked and where it is left alone.

FLIGHT DISTANCES

Many wild creatures, especially birds will allow an enemy to approach to within a certain distance of them before they move away. This distance is known as the *flight distance*. Measure the flight distances of different species of birds as accurately as possible in your garden and note where the birds go to. Calculate the average distance for a number of observations of the same species in your garden. Carry out similar observations in other localities, such as playing fields, parks, public gardens and the open countryside; compare these results with those obtained in your garden. By how much can the flight distance be reduced by putting out food? Do the flight distances for any given species vary according to the season of the year?

SUN-BATHING

Although sun-bathing is a widespread habit of birds, it is one about which there are many gaps in our knowledge. We are not even certain why birds sunbathe. Many reasons have been put forward; among them that the bird is striving to lose heat, as indeed it is during very hot weather. But birds also sun-bathe in the winter. The sunshine may stimulate the preen gland just above the bird's tail to activity, or it may stimulate the skin to produce vitamin D, as happens with humans. Another suggestion is that the warmth of the sun causes parasites to move to the surface of the plumage where they can be picked off by the infected bird.

Fig. 17. Blackbird sunbathing

To help to answer these questions you should record the species and number of any birds that you see sun-bathing, together with the place, date, weather conditions (particularly the temperature and position of the sun), and time of the day. Make notes on the posture of the bird, paying particular attention to the position of the head, tail and wings, and note whether the eyes were open or closed. Do different species adopt different postures, and do the postures vary with the weather conditions?

BATHING

Most birds bathe, not so much to cleanse their feathers, but rather to allow proper preening to take place. Again this is a subject about which we need to know a great deal more.

Record all instances of bathing and try and find out if different species adopt different methods of wetting themselves. What is the preferred depth of water for each species? This can be found out by offering a series of identical containers filled with water to different depths, or else a bath with a gradually sloping base, in which case you will be able to note how far the bird is from the edge.

What water temperatures do birds prefer? Offer them a series of containers, filled to the same depth with water at different temperatures, say 10°C, 20°C, 30°C and 40°C. On no account use water which is above 40°C or the bird may be scalded. The larger the containers used, the longer will the water hold its temperature.

Record the air temperature whenever you see birds bathing. Note also the natural water temperature of the bird bath, and the time of day when they are bathing. Do birds have a favourite bath-time? Describe how they dry and preen themselves after bathing. By looking for individuals with distinctive plumage such as a blackbird with one or two white feathers can you find out how often a bird bathes?

ANTING

Anting is the term used for an astonishing pattern of behaviour shown by many passerine birds. In it the bird either allows ants to crawl over its body, usually worker ants of the species which secrete formic acid, or actually applies them to its plumage, mostly to the inner side of its wings and tail quills.

The function of anting is unknown. It is possible that the formic acid from the ants may kill or discourage parasites on the plumage, or it may be that certain oils from the ants have a beneficial effect on the feathers. Unlike dust- and water-bathing, not all birds of a species known to ant seem to do it. Some do it occasionally, some do it frequently, others never seem to ant. There is much still to be discovered about this strange behaviour and careful records should be made of any examples of it that you may see.

Fig. 18. Birds bathing

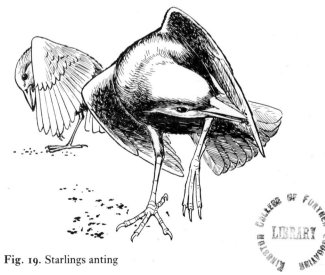

Fig. 19. Starlings anting

KINGSTON COLLEGE OF FURTHER EDUCATION LIBRARY

It is difficult to see anting under natural conditions but you can be fairly certain of seeing it if you collect half a bucket of ants, particularly the large wood ants from plantations of conifers, and on a sunny day tip them out on a dust bath (see page 41), a lawn, near a bird table, or in any place where many wild birds regularly congregate. Attract the birds to the ants, if needs be, with a supply of food. Watch from a window or some other vantage point. Starlings are most likely to ant, but you may have the luck to see a jay, chaffinch, song thrush or some other species do it.

Incidentally, a small number of birds go through the motions of anting, not with ants but with such strange objects as strong-smelling fruits, burning pieces of twig or even lighted cigarette ends. All such incidents should be recorded in detail.

Fig. 20. Jackdaw smoke-bathing

restricted to certain species, or that preference is shown for certain types of smoke?

SMOKE-BATHING

Smoke-bathing is another strange habit of some birds. Birds sometimes can be seen cavorting in a current of smoke, such as that from a chimney. We do not properly understand the reasons for smoke-bathing but they probably have something to do with the chemicals in the smoke, which perhaps reduce the number of parasites or cause them to move to the surface of the bird's body from where they can be removed.

Keep accurate records, which must include the species, the postures adopted and the type of fuel that produced the smoke.

Is there any evidence to show that smoke-bathing is

MOULTING

Collect the feathers scattered from week to week in a place where flocks of birds gather. Mount each week's collection on card and, by comparing the various cards, reconstruct the order in which the different types of feathers are moulted.

RIGHT-FOOTED BIRDS AND LEFT-FOOTED BIRDS

Most humans are right-handed in their day to day activities; a far smaller number use the left hand regularly. No one seems to have made a study of which foot birds use in their daily life.

Record carefully all instances where you see birds use their feet to hold food, to dig or scratch themselves, etc. Does a clear picture of right-footed or left-footed predominance of the various species emerge? In other words, are there right-footed birds or left-footed birds, or do they use whichever foot happens to suit them at any given time?

SEED DISPERSAL BY BIRDS

Quite a large number of plant seeds are dispersed by birds in their droppings. An examination of the ground below a woodland starling roost will often reveal a number of unusual plants, sometimes plants from overseas, which have grown from seeds that have passed through the birds' body undigested.

You might experiment by spreading the droppings of birds (collected with an old spoon) in plant pots full of soil that has been baked in the oven to kill any seeds it may have contained. Water the soil regularly. Any plants that now grow will have come from seeds present in the bird droppings. Try and identify the seedlings and make a table showing which plants are dispersed by each of the birds whose droppings have been examined.

road accident victims. This can be done on any stretch of busy road that you travel along regularly, perhaps on your way to school each day.

Every day record the number and species of birds that you find dead along your stretch of road and, if you have a map of the road, mark on it where each accident victim was found. Pay particular attention to whether the birds are juveniles or adults.

In which month or months are most birds killed? Which species is the most frequent victim? Do young birds form a large proportion of the casualties during the summer months? Are there any features such as a wall, hedge or tall tree by the roadside, or perhaps a gap between two large buildings: do such features affect the numbers of birds killed? Are more birds killed during periods when visibility is poor such as in mist, fog or heavy rain? Are more birds killed during the early morning (count on your way to school), than are killed during the rest of the day (count again in the evening on your way home)?

If possible, compare the results that you obtain on a busy town road with those from a country road that carries fast-moving traffic, or perhaps you can exchange results with a friend. Can you find any evidence that town birds have more road sense than country birds?

ROAD ACCIDENT VICTIMS

It is estimated that every year about $2\frac{1}{2}$ million birds are killed on Britain's roads and an interesting if somewhat sad project is to carry out a survey of these

BIRD CORPSES

How are the corpses of birds disposed of in nature? After all, one rarely comes across the corpses of birds that have been in position a long time.

To help to answer this question, obtain the body of a dead bird. Road accident victims are the easiest to find, but do not touch the corpse with your hands. Instead, carefully sweep it onto the blade of a trowel or spade. Lay the corpse on the surface of the soil in an out-of-the-way part of the garden and protect it from cats by covering it with a cloche or a tent of wire netting.

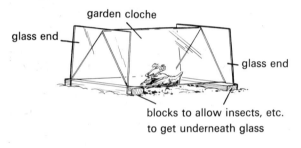

Fig. 21. An experiment on the disposal of a dead blackbird in nature

How long does the corpse take to disappear? Try and identify the various kinds of insects, mainly beetles and the maggots of two-winged flies, responsible for its removal. Samples of the maggots living in the corpse can be removed from time to time, using forceps, and kept in tins or jars of soil covered with a piece of old stocking until they pupate. Eventually the flies will hatch out when they can be identified, using a reference book such as **The Oxford Book of Insects** by J. Burton.

Lay another corpse in a prominent place and keep watch on it from a distance for a period of several hours. What species of birds and mammals feed on such carrion? If you are able to, you might repeat this observation at night using a torch covered with a piece of red cellophane. Most nocturnal creatures have eyes which are insensitive to red light; you will be able to observe them although they will not be aware of your presence if you keep still.

BIRD STRIKES

Reports of birds flying into windows, even being killed by the impact, are quite common. There are several possible reasons for these accidents. The bird may be attracted by something in the room, or it may see its own reflection, which it then tries to attack. It may see the reflection of something outside in the garden such as a bird table or bird bath which it tries to fly to. Another possibility is that crashes occur where there is a window at the opposite end of the room. If both windows are large, the bird may crash if it tries to fly straight through the imagined open space to the daylight it can see.

You can obviously help to increase your knowledge of these bird strikes if you keep records of all such accidents, but you can learn even more if you carry out a survey of all the strikes which occur in the neighbourhood. Ask your friends, neighbours, and school-mates, to tell you of any such accidents. Record the species involved and note whether or not the bird recovered. Was the bird involved an adult or a juvenile? Describe where the accident occurred and the weather conditions, particularly the wind strength and direction, visibility, and position of the sun. Suggest also possible reasons for each strike. What is the most common cause of these accidents to birds?

DIVING

This project is unlikely to be possible in the ordinary garden, but it can be undertaken in parks and public gardens which have an ornamental lake. Ideally a stopwatch or a watch with a second hand is required, although you can get by, merely by counting.

Different species of diving birds such as tufted ducks, coots and grebes, seem to stay under water for greatly varying lengths of time. Time a number of dives for each of the species being studied and find the average. It is possible that the length of the dive may also depend upon the depth of the water, so if you can compare the average length of time the different species stay submerged in two areas where the water depths differ, you might be able to find out if this is an important factor.

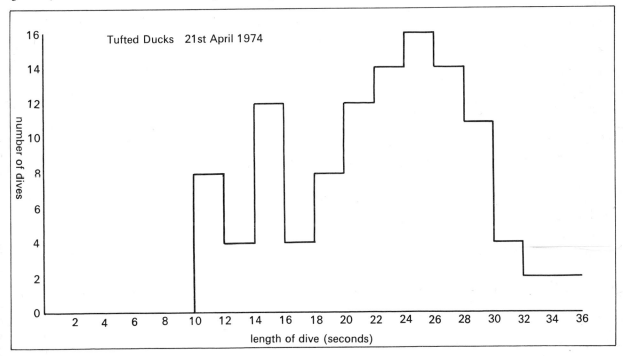

Fig. 22. Results of a study of diving birds

CHAPTER SIX

More Difficult Projects

PHOTOGRAPHING BIRDS

Dozens of birds visit your garden every day and you can learn to photograph them if you are able to overcome the two basic problems. The first of these problems is how to get close enough to the bird and, secondly, because the bird is so small, how to get a picture of it large enough to show the detail of the plumage.

Fig. 1. An expert bird photographer at work

The expert bird photographer uses one of two methods to get close enough to the bird.

One is the 'wait and see' method, by which the camera is set up inside a hide (see page 16), close to one of the focal points for birds such as a bird table, drinking pool or singing post and the photographer waits for the birds to arrive. The second method is to stalk the bird using a camera fitted with a telephoto lens: a similar principle to fitting a telescope to the front of the camera.

What kind of camera is needed for bird photography? The ordinary box camera or 'Instamatic' camera is not really suitable for taking pictures of smaller birds. The reason is that the focal length of the lens fitted to these simple cameras only projects a small image onto the film. Even if you could get to within 60 to 100 cm of the bird, the image would still be very small, and there is no means of fitting other lenses or of controlling the shutter speed sufficiently to *stop* the bird. Such cameras as these can give good results if one keeps to the larger species such as ducks, geese and swans and they are also useful for taking pictures of the habitats of birds.

A good basic camera for bird photography is the 35 mm camera, and the type now used almost universally is the single lens reflex camera. This type of camera is intricately made, and has shutter speeds as fast as 1/500 or even 1/1000 of a second. Such cameras are reasonably lightweight for their size and can easily be fitted with a wide range of telephoto lenses of different powers. Their outstanding advantage, however, is that they have a viewfinder which opens out into the lens at the front of the camera, so that when you look into the viewfinder you see exactly what the camera lens is seeing.

The advantage of 35 mm cameras in general is that film is reasonably cheap and buying colour film is more economical in this small size; the film comes in special light-proof cassettes which contain enough for 20 or 36 exposures.

I must emphasize here that, even if they are bought second-hand, good single lens reflex cameras are expensive. Most 35 mm cameras are fitted with a 50 mm lens for general photography, but for stalking birds or taking pictures of them from a hide, a telephoto lens of about 200 or 300 mm focal length is generally recommended. This will probably cost as much, perhaps even more, than the camera. If you cannot afford a single reflex camera and telephoto lens, and most young people cannot, you can still photograph birds if you have a camera—preferably a 35 mm which has a range of shutter speeds up to at least 1/200 of a second, a number of apertures to $f5\cdot6$ or larger (the larger the aperture the smaller the f number, thus $f2\cdot8$ is a much larger aperture than $f8$ or $f11$), and the means to fit a cable release to the shutter and a close-up lens to the front of the main lens.

It takes an expert photographer to estimate the correct shutter speed according to the strength of light and the speed of film. An exposure meter or exposure calculator is therefore, a valuable additional aid and it will soon pay for itself in savings on film that you would otherwise waste.

Only experience and patience will produce pleasing photographs. Begin by including general views of the

PLATE X. Take a lesson from the birds: by keeping still and because of her markings, this hen pheasant is almost invisible

habitats of birds and other related subjects; trees, flowers, your friends bird-watching, and so on. All this will give practice in the use of your camera and film and you will quickly become familiar with your equipment.

The technique of bird photography that I describe is ideal for use in the garden. It involves no disturbance, or cruelty to the birds and is much less expensive than traditional forms of bird photography. If you choose wisely your whole collection of equipment will cost you no more than a pair of Japanese binoculars of reasonable quality. What is more, is that this technique can give good results even with inexpensive equipment.

For this method of bird photography you will need to use a fast film: a 400 ASA black-and-white film or a 160 to 200 ASA colour film. The speed of a film is printed on the side of the packet, and if you are in doubt your photographic dealer will be able to help you.

You will also need a two diopter close-up lens, which can be purchased quite cheaply, a tape measure, a lens hood for your camera, a tripod and a pneumatic air release. A pneumatic air release is a length of very thin rubber or plastic tubing attached to a rubber bulb with a firing mechanism at the other end. Pressure on the bulb releases the shutter of your camera from a distance. Pneumatic releases are available in various lengths from 6 metres to about 25 metres. Buy the longest one you can afford. All these pieces of equipment are useful for other types of photographic work; the close-up lens can be used for table-top photography, photographing plants, and many other things; the pneumatic release is particularly useful for photographing young children and pets in natural poses and for taking photographs of yourself.

A few days before taking the photographs, select a suitable site to erect an old rustic post as a stage on which the birds can pose for you. When choosing the site, take careful note of the background behind your subject. Watch for dark shadows which will spoil

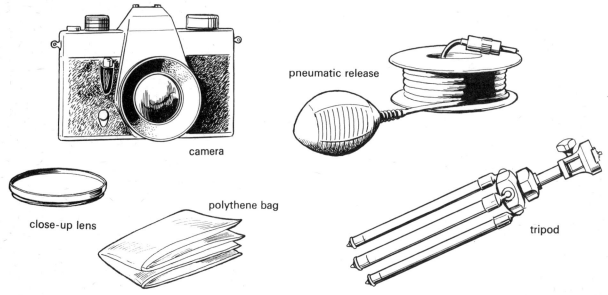

camera

pneumatic release

close-up lens

polythene bag

tripod

Fig. 2. What you need for bird photography in the garden

polythene bag over camera

bulb of air release

Fig. 3. Bird photography with a pneumatic camera release

your photograph. Leave some food on and around the post for several days so that the birds become used to settling on this spot and will come there for food.

When the day comes to take your photographs, set up your equipment in the following way: load the film in the camera, put the camera on the tripod and fit the close-up lens and hood to the camera. Take your camera into the garden and set it up, with the camera pointing at the post, so that the area covered by the lens, as seen through the viewfinder, is about 35 cm wide. Remember also that unless your camera is a single lens reflex, at this close distance you must allow for the fact that the viewfinder and camera lens are not looking at the object at quite the same angle.

When you look through the viewfinder, imagine there is a bird standing on top of the post, and then move the camera up slightly so that there is a space of about 9 or 10 cm above its head. If you fail to do this you may find that in your photographs the bird's head has been chopped off!

Attach the pneumatic air release to the camera and with your two diopter close-up lens in place, set the focus scale to infinity and position the camera so that from the front of the close-up lens to the centre of the top of the post is exactly 50 cm. When setting the exposure, remember that you need an aperture of f11 to f16 to get even a small depth of field so that all of the bird is in focus. A speed of 1/125 to 1/200 of a second is quite adequate for photographing birds in this way, because at the time of exposure the bird is stationary.

Put a piece of fat or suitable bait on the post to tempt the birds to alight; if you want your photograph to look even more natural, sprinkle bread crumbs on the ground around the post.

Set the shutter, being very careful not to jog the camera, and then cover the camera with a clean polythene bag, in which you have cut holes for the lens and pneumatic release. Secure the bag by using either Sellotape or elastic bands. The purpose of the polythene bag is to avoid any damage to the camera should the birds decide to sit on it, or if there is a sudden rain shower.

Pick up the bulb of the air release and take it to a suitable vantage point (Fig. 3). This can be either a chair behind a bush or some other suitable background, from where you can see the birds, and they cannot see you. If the day is cold, you can pass the end of the air release through an open window and sit indoors in comfort, keeping an eye on the birds through the window.

It may take some time for the birds to come because they will be wary of the camera. In the meantime you must keep a watch on the sky to see that the light conditions do not change; if they do you will have to alter the exposure setting on the camera. When the birds do begin to settle and take the food, do not be in a hurry to shoot as soon as one lands on the post, wait until you have the bird in exactly the right position for your photograph. As soon as the bird hears your shutter click it will fly off, and it may be ten or fifteen minutes before it returns. This will give you time to wind on the film and re-set the shutter.

When you have the film developed, or if you do it yourself, see that a fine grain developer is used to give maximum detail on the negative. If the negatives are printed on to glossy bromide paper they will have extra brilliance.

This technique, using the close-up lens, can also be used to photograph a robin sitting on the handle of a spade, a bird at a song-post, or a blue or great tit feeding on a peanut stuck in the bark of a tree. If you choose a still day, and use the fastest available shutter speed, you can photograph tits feeding on a string of peanuts or at a feeding basket.

Without the close-up lens, and at a distance of one metre or more, you can photograph birds feeding at the bird table or drinking or bathing at a small pool. When adjusting the focus of the lens I find it useful to place a small white pebble at the spot where the bird will be standing when I press the air release.

No mention has been made of photographing birds at their nests. In the past, many photographs have been taken of nesting birds as the nest acts as a focal point to which the birds are drawn to feed the young or brood the eggs. Unless great care is used and the photographer has expert knowledge, it is extremely dangerous to attempt to photograph birds at the nest, because of the dangers of the bird deserting or of exposing the eggs or young to predators. It is now illegal to photograph most birds at the nest without a licence from the Nature Conservancy.

The technique described in this chapter can be applied the year round, and there is always the thrill and excitement of a rare bird coming and sitting in front of your camera.

RECORDING BIRD-SONG

To some extent, the recording of bird-song is like bird photography; the more money you have to spend on it, the greater the scope you will have. Nevertheless, satisfactory recordings can be made on quite inexpensive tape recorders, which will enable you to carry out a whole range of fascinating studies of bird-song.

A portable tape recorder obviously enables the bird-watcher to study a far greater range of species, but even a recorder operated from the household mains circuit can produce interesting tapes. A mains tape recorder can be operated from a car battery if you use a device known as a vibrator converter. In this case the field of operation is limited only by the length of the cable attached to the recorder.

If you are choosing a new machine, remember that a heavy one will be cumbersome to carry and will limit your activities. The running time per spool of tape is very important, for it is most frustrating to have the tape run out in the middle of what might have been an excellent recording. This also applies to the battery life if the recorder is a portable one. The quality of reproduction and the speed of the tape, the other two factors to be considered, can be dealt with together. In general, the faster the tape speed, the truer the sound recorded, and also, unfortunately, the higher the running costs and the more expensive the machine to buy.

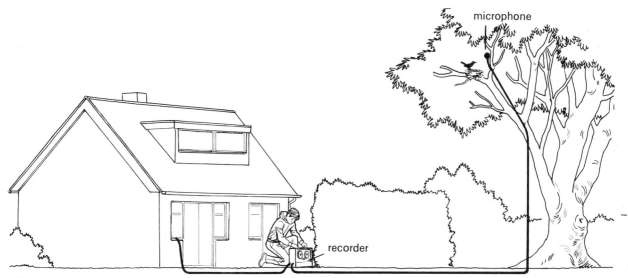

Fig. 4. Recording bird song

One piece of equipment used by most serious recordists of bird-song is a parabolic reflector. This is a device rather like a large shallow basin made of metal which can be beamed towards the singing bird, and operates like a huge mechanical ear, collecting the sound and directing it into the microphone. It enables a bird's song to be recorded at up to 40 times the distance normally possible.

You have no need to bother about a parabolic reflector until you have gained a great deal of experience, but it is something to consider for the future.

As in all forms of bird study, patience is essential in recording bird-song. You must wait for a calm dry day before recording. Wind will upset the microphone, causing it to vibrate, and may also set the cable swinging, which will add further to the unwanted background noise. The sound of traffic is very annoying and irritating in a recording, so you should set up your apparatus as far from the road as possible, or in the early morning before the traffic is heavy and when the bird activity is greatest. Incidentally, the best recordings are those made with the volume control on the tape recorder turned low. Recording at a high volume produces distortion of the bird's song.

What sort of things can you record? One of the easiest and most pleasant sounds to tape is the dawn chorus. You need not even get out of bed to do this, but can stand the microphone on the outside window-sill and switch on the machine from your bed.

The territorial songs of the common species can be recorded by placing the microphone near one of their song-posts and waiting quietly. Usually the bird will return to a particular position to sing. If it goes some distance away and sings, tape it, and then replay the recording as loudly as possible. Quite often the bird will return to its original song-post and sing again, loudly. You can now record this song and erase the original and more distant one; using this technique you will gradually be able to build up a tape library of bird-songs which is a great aid to identification.

You may want to build up a set of recordings of all the calls and songs of an individual species. This is an excellent subject for study since fewer than twenty of the 200 or so common British birds have had their complete vocabularies recorded. Two species well worth study in this respect are the rook and the house sparrow.

If you get the chance to travel around the country a lot, or if you have friends with whom you could swap tapes, you might find it profitable to study the local dialects of a bird such as the chaffinch. This is not to suggest that there is such a thing as a chaffinch with a Yorkshire accent, but by comparing tapes you might well find that the chaffinches from one part of the country have a slightly different song from those from another.

One of the most amusing experiments is to play back the recorded sound of a bird in its own territory. It will assume the song is that of an intruder, and an aggressive bird, such as a robin, may even attack the tape recorder. Most birds will then break into vigorous song, incensed that another bird has dared to enter their territory.

Similarly, you can play back the alarm calls of a bird, such as those made when a cat is on the prowl,

Fig. 5. Playing back the recorded sound of a bird in its own territory

and watch the results. Another interesting experiment is to play the call of the predator, such as a tawny owl, and see what happens. Neither of these experiments should be carried out in the breeding season though, since you will certainly distress those birds with eggs or young and may cause the nest to be deserted.

Much can be learnt too, from replaying taped bird-songs at a speed slower than the recording speed. Birds hear sounds faster than humans, picking out details of song which are too rapid for the human ear to distinguish. Only by slowing down the recording can you hear the song as the bird probably hears it. The song of a swift, for instance, is a high-pitched screech to the human ear, but slowed down, the sound is heard as a melodious warble with distinct notes.

Interesting as these experiments are, the greatest pleasure in recording bird-song comes from its beauty. What better way of spending a cold winter's evening than listening to the song of a cuckoo or nightingale, and thinking of the warmer weather to come?

RINGING BIRDS

People have been ringing birds for a long time for various reasons. According to that great eighteenth century naturalist, Gilbert White of Selborne, a duck was shot during the winter of 1708-9 bearing a silver collar round its neck engraved with the arms of the King of Denmark. This early example of bird marking was to demonstrate ownership, rather than for a scientific purpose.

Bird ringing as we know it today, began in Denmark at the end of the last century and started in Britain in 1909. Since that time more than 6 million birds have been ringed here, and information has been recovered about some 170,000 of them.

Not only does ringing tell us about the migratory habits of birds, it also gives us information about the speeds at which they travel whilst on migration, and the age to which a bird may live.

A few years ago, an arctic tern breeding on the Farne Islands was found to be wearing a ring that showed it was 27 years old. During its lifetime it must have travelled well over 2 million miles on its twice-yearly migrations.

An example of the incredible speed at which some birds travel over vast oceans was shown by some Manx shearwaters ringed in their breeding burrows on Skokholm Island off the coast of Wales before they were old enough to fly. Six weeks later they were recovered in Brazil after completing a journey of 4,500 miles.

Only a small proportion of ringed birds are ever seen again. The recovery rate is highest for large birds such as swans, geese and the birds of prey, and lowest for the small song birds, many of which spend winter in remote parts of Africa.

The majority of the larger countries of the world now have a national scheme for marking birds by the leg-ringing method. The British scheme is operated through the British Trust for Ornithology which supplies a diverse range of bird rings, from the smallest, suitable for a goldcrest or the small warblers, which has an inside diameter of only 2 mm, to the largest, a swan ring, with an inside measurement of 26 mm.

Before it is put on the bird, the ring, which is made of a light aluminium alloy, is in the form of a strip. It is then closed round the bird's leg and when applied properly, a task which calls for skill and experience, it will not harm or discomfort the bird.

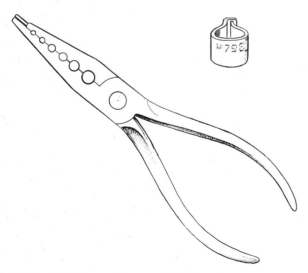

Fig. 6. A bird ring and the specially designed pliers used to put a ring onto a bird's leg

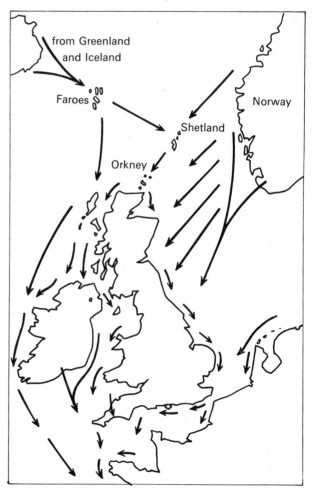

Fig. 7. The main paths of the autumn migration of birds along the shores of Britain

The British rings bear a serial number and the words: 'Inform British Museum, London S.W.7' (the address of the Natural History Museum in South Kensington, London). If the ring is small the word 'Inform' is omitted.

If you find a dead bird anywhere, no matter how decayed it may be, look for the ring on its leg. It may produce interesting information as did the redwing, ringed in Norway as a nestling, and found dead by the roadside four years later in Hertfordshire. If the ring is a metal one of the type just described, the ends should be visible. Remove the ring from the bird and send it, together with your name and address, the date and place you found the bird, and any other details of interest to:

British Museum (Natural History),
South Kensington,
London, S.W.7.

Even if the ring is a foreign one, still send it to the British Museum and they will forward the details to the authorities in the appropriate country. You will later be informed where the bird was ringed.

Sometimes a different kind of ring is found. It has no end showing and usually has a rimmed edge. This sort of ring, which bears only a number, is from a racing pigeon and should be sent to:

The National Homing Union,
22, Clarence Street,
Gloucester.

Any other rings, including coloured ones, should be ignored. They are normally the type used by local naturalists to identify individual birds, and cannot be traced.

The ringed birds that you find, however, may not always be dead ones. Birds on migration sometimes fly into buildings by mistake or become so exhausted that they cannot fly any further and are easily caught. If you find such a bird that is ringed, do not attempt to take the ring off; you will spoil any chance of further recoveries and may well injure the bird's fragile legs in the process.

Fig. 8. How to hold a bird to examine a ring

Large birds are quite sturdily built, but small ones need careful handling. Do not grab wildly at the bird but instead use the fingers of one hand to form a 'cage' to secure the bird so that it cannot flap (Fig. 8). Be especially careful not to press against the bird's fragile ribs or you will damage its internal organs.

Hold the bird so that its head sticks out from the 'cage' between your index and middle fingers and with your other hand gently draw out the leg which is ringed. You can then send the details concerning the bird and its ring to the British Museum.

Before you release the bird to continue its journey, try and tempt it to regain its strength with some sultanas or bread-and-milk, and a dish of water.

I have already said that putting a ring on a bird's leg calls for a great deal of skill and that careless handling of the bird can injure it. For this reason, the official numbered rings issued by the British Trust for Ornithology can only be used by a ringer who is licensed by the B.T.O.

To learn how to ring birds it is essential to gain experience under the supervision of a B.T.O. licensed ringer who is recognized as a trainer, and you must also prove yourself to be an expert at identification. One of the best and most exciting ways of gaining such experience is to stay at one of the observatories around our coasts where the marking of hundreds of migrating birds takes place from spring to autumn. The B.T.O. will send you a list of observatories on receipt of a stamped addressed envelope.

The earliest age at which you can receive a licence to ring birds is 16 years. However any keen young bird-watcher may ring birds provided it is done under the direct supervision of someone who is himself a licensed ringer. Your local natural history society may be able to put you in touch with a licensed ringer in your area, if this is not possible then the B.T.O. will help you, but do not waste their valuable time unless you are seriously interested in training to become a ringer.

CHAPTER SEVEN

Making a Species Study

After you have carried out some of the projects described in the preceding chapters, and when you have gained a fair knowledge of birds in general, you might like to make a species study. This involves getting to know everything that can be learnt about the various aspects that go to make up the life of the bird you have selected; its feeding, song, flight, roosting habits, breeding behaviour, and so on. The species study will in fact use much of the information already collected in earlier projects.

It is wise to choose a species which is reasonably common in your area. A species seen only occasionally may be interesting or exciting, but one just cannot learn enough about it to make a life history study worthwhile. It may seem rather dull to go for a common bird, but it is surprising how much there is still to be learnt about even our most familiar creatures.

You might also begin with a species which is present throughout the year, otherwise you will find that for several months you have little that you can do, and your interest may wane.

Another point that you might bear in mind when choosing a species for study is that unless you are able to mark birds with coloured leg bands to distinguish them, you would be wise to study first a species such as the blackbird, chaffinch or house sparrow, in which the sexes can easily be distinguished.

Having chosen your species to study, a number of other points are important for success. First you must work upon it steadily and watch regularly. In the spring and summer months in particular, it is essential to get up early. Breeding birds begin their activities at dawn, sometimes before dawn, and they are most interesting to watch during the morning as they sing and search for food. By midday they are often fully fed, and more inclined to rest, which makes observation difficult.

As in every kind of study, the first essential is regular and careful note-taking, and the field note-book should always be kept in the pocket. Record every detail, however trivial, of the activity of the chosen species. Always put in too much rather than too little. Any detail that turns out to be unimportant can always be left out later from your permanent record. Incidentally, for the species study in particular, a card index is extremely useful for your permanent record, with one card devoted to 'Nest Sites', another to 'Food', another to 'Roosting', and so on.

One of your first tasks, is to find out as much as you can from reference books about your chosen species. Keep notes of the more important points, together with details of the page and title of the book in which they were found. Do not accept any fact as being absolutely correct; check each detail, as far as you can, against your own observations.

As a guide to making a species study along the lines mentioned here, I have included a list of questions for you to try and answer. No doubt many more will come to you as your work proceeds. Some of these queries will be difficult and may take several years' observation to answer satisfactorily. Nevertheless, if you only answer some of them, you will gain much knowledge from doing so.

Before you start a species study, I would ask you to read again the precautions mentioned on page 48 about visiting birds' nests, and on page 83 about studying their roosting habits.

APPEARANCE, STRUCTURE, ETC.

What colour is the bird? Is there very much variation in colour between the different members of the species?

Are the bills the same colour all the year?

How are male and female distinguished?

When and where does the bird moult? How can you recognize a bird that has recently moulted and renewed its plumage?

When do you see tailless birds?

Can the bird grip a vertical branch?

FOOD AND FEEDING

Which of a range of foods you supply does the bird prefer?

What are its natural foods?

Can the bird catch insects on the wing?

Can it hold down a piece of food with one foot to peck at it?

Will it go into a dark place for food?

Is the bird harmful to garden plants or farm crops?

If so, which plants are harmed, when, and are they harmed for food or nesting material?

Does the bird prefer the cover of bushes for ground foraging?

Does it ever find food in trees (a) naturally, (b) when you put it there?

Can it take food fastened to a really thin branch, hung on a string, or stuck in the bark of a tree?

When food is suspended from a string, can the bird haul up the food to the level of the perch?

Does the bird turn over leaves or stones to find food (a) naturally, (b) when you have put it there?

Does the bird eat any kind of grit?

Does it make a special call to signal to others of its kind that food is about?

ROOSTING

At what time does the bird go to bed? Is it the same time throughout the year?

Does the bird wake up at the same time each day? Is it earlier or later than other species?

Where does the bird roost in (a) the breeding season, (b) the rest of the year?

Does the bird roost singly or in groups?

MOVEMENT

Does the bird ever glide in flight?

Does it fly in a straight line or does it follow an up-and-down path?

Where are the feet during flight?

Does the bird come out (a) during light rain, or (b) during heavy rain, or does it come out immediately after rain?

If the bird is found in flocks, do the flocks have a regular route of progress round the district?

Does the bird walk when on the ground, or hop or run?

BATHING, GROOMING, ETC.

What movements does the bird make when bathing in water or dust?

Does the bird bathe alone or in flocks?

Are there special scouts to warn of danger if the birds bathe in groups?

How do various weather conditions, particularly temperature, affect bathing activity?

Will the bird use a fountain or lawn sprinkler if this is provided in hot weather?

What parts of the bird are groomed, (a) with the beak, (b) with the feet?

Does the bird groom itself on the ground?

How are the head and beak groomed?

Does the bird sunbathe? If so, when, where, and alone or in the company of other birds?

COURTSHIP AND TERRITORY

How big is the bird's territory?

Does the bird feed outside its breeding territory?

How does the bird obtain its territory?

How are trespassers dealt with?

How does the bird defend its territory, and against whom?

How do the pair behave during courtship?

Where are the singing posts in the territory?

When and where does mating take place?

How do the mated birds recognize each other?

If the species is resident, when does each adult take up its winter territory? Or flock?

When do the young birds of the year acquire a territory?

NESTING AND BREEDING

How is the nest site chosen? By one or both birds?

What sites are chosen for the nest?

Which of the pair builds the nest?

What kind of materials are used for the nest and from where are they obtained?

How long does nest-building take?

How many eggs are laid, and when?

Do the eggs all hatch the same day, or at intervals?

Is the incubation of the eggs shared by both birds?

Is the incubating bird fed by its mate?

How and where are the egg-shells disposed of after hatching?

For how long are the nestlings brooded continuously after they are hatched? And how often, and when, later on?

How do the parent birds assure that their offspring receive fair shares of the food?

How often are the nestlings fed? And on what?

How and where are the nestlings' droppings disposed of?

What call notes and other noises do the nestlings make throughout their life in the nest?

When does the nestling first open its eyes? Grow the first down? Sprout its first feathers? First beat its wings? Walk? Climb? Leave the nest?

Do the parents encourage the young to leave the nest? How?

Where do the young birds roost?

Do the young birds keep together when they first leave the nest, or do they scatter widely?

For how long do the parents continue to feed the young?

How do the young birds develop their powers of flight?

What enemies do the young birds have?

Are the young birds eventually driven away by their parents?

When do the young birds moult? When do they achieve the adult plumage?

Is there a second or even a third brood?

Do the breeding pair remain together for life? If not, what happens to them?

MIGRATION

Do the numbers increase in winter or summer? Is there evidence of migration?

Where do the birds migrate to? When do they leave? When do they arrive back?

Do the young birds leave before the adults?

Do the birds migrate singly, in family groups, or in large flocks?

GENERAL BEHAVIOUR

How many birds do you commonly see together? Do you ever see one or two alone, apart from in the breeding season?

Which birds drive away your selected species?

And which are driven away by it?

Does it give warning calls of danger? If so, describe them?

What calls and songs are made throughout the year?

Is there any evidence of anting?

Study the behaviour of individuals in a flock. Which individuals are dominant? How do they dominate the others?

How does the bird react to stuffed predators such as owls, hawks, stoats, etc.?

Bird Books

Bird-watching is not an expensive hobby. In a way it is rather like a stamp collection, in that it can be almost as cheap and certainly as costly as you like. This is definitely true of your collection of bird books. The list given overleaf is not meant to be a comprehensive and final one. It is absolutely essential to have a good book on the identification of British birds; others are a matter of taste and interest.

You will notice also that I have not kept strictly to the title of this section, but have included books on flowering plants, trees and shrubs, insects, the weather, and other topics. Many bird-watchers make the mistake of having too many books on birds and not enough books to which they can refer in order to identify bird foods, nesting sites, nesting materials, the contents of pellets, and so on. This is an attempt to remedy this deficiency.

Some of the books in this list are now out of print, a few of them are very expensive and out of reach of your pocket money, some of them you may only want to refer to once or twice and then not look at again. Do not let these things worry you, since you can always make use of the local library.

Every town in Britain has a public library, and almost every village is visited by a mobile library or has a small branch in the village or church hall, school, or some other place.

Most libraries of reasonable size are arranged in at least three departments: **Children's Library** for young people under the age of 14 years, a **Lending Library** meant for adults but which young people can also use if they wish, and a **Reference Library**.

The two Lending Libraries, the children's and adults' are arranged according to the same system with the story books and novels separated from the information books. Story books and novels make up the Fiction section of the library, information books, including bird books and general natural history books, are in the Non-Fiction section.

In the Non-Fiction section you will find that all books on the same subject have been collected together and given a number which is embossed on the spine of the book. This is to make it easier to find and replace the books in the correct position on the shelves. Most public libraries use a system called the Dewey Decimal Classification in which the number for the subject **Birds** is 598.2.

If you cannot find the book you want, or indeed if you cannot find the section on birds, ask one of the librarians to help you. Of course it may be that the library has not got the particular book that you want to read in its stocks. In that case, if you fill in one of the special Book Request Cards that the librarian will give you, the book will either be purchased or borrowed from another library, and you will be informed when it is ready for you to collect.

The Reference Library does not lend out its books and so they are always there for you to refer to. It includes rare and valuable books, encyclopedias as well as quick reference books and standard books in all subjects. An invaluable reference work, **The Handbook of British Birds** is almost certain to be in the Reference Library. The regulations concerning the use of Reference Libraries vary from one place to another and, to be on the safe side, always ask the librarian if you may use it. No serious request for information is likely to be refused.

GENERAL BIRD BOOKS

Nestboxes, E. Cohen (British Trust for Ornithology).

British Garden Birds (includes 2 gramophone records), P. Conder.

Shell Bird Book, J. Fisher (Ebury Press).

The World of Birds, J. Fisher and R.T. Peterson (MacDonald).

Book of British Birds, R. Fitter (editor) (Drive Publications).

The Bird Garden, P.H.T. Hartley (Royal Society for the Protection of Birds).

Birds as Living Things, M. Knight (Routledge).

Enjoying Ornithology, D. Lack (Methuen).

Treatment of Sick and Wounded Birds, F.B. Lack (British Trust for Ornithology).

Wild Birds and the Land, F.H. Lancum (H.M.S.O.).

A New Dictionary of Birds, A. Landsborough-Thompson (Nelson).

A Bird and its Bush, M. Lister (Phoenix).

Bird Biology, J.D. Macdonald (Museum Press).

Bird Life in the Royal Parks, Ministry of Public Buildings and Works (H.M.S.O.).

Birds and Men, E.M. Nicholson (Collins).

The Bird Table Book, T. Soper (David and Charles).

Bird Life, N. Tinbergen (Oxford).

The Handbook of British Birds, H. Witherby etc. (Witherby).

Birds and Woods, W.B. Yapp (Oxford).

IDENTIFICATION

The Observer's Book of British Birds, S.V. Benson (Warne).

The Hamlyn Guide to the Birds of Britain and Europe, B. Bruun (Hamlyn).

The Oxford Book of Birds, B. Campbell and D. Watson (Oxford).

The Birds of the British Isles and their Eggs, T.A. Coward (Warne).

The Pocket Guide to British Birds, R.S.R. Fitter (Collins).

The Pocket Guide to Eggs and Nests, R.S.R. Fitter (Collins).

Birds' Nests and Eggs, C.J.O. Harrison (Museum Press).

Bird Spotting, J. Holland (Blandford).

The Popular Handbook of British Birds, P. Hollom (Witherby).

A Field Guide to the Birds of Britain and Europe, R.T. Peterson, G. Mountford and P. Hollom (Collins).

BIRD-WATCHING

Bird Watching as a Hobby, W.D. Campbell (S. Paul).

Bird Watching, P. Clarke (Newnes).

Birdwatching, E.A.R. Ennion (M. Joseph).

Guide to Birdwatching, R.S.R. Fitter (Collins).

Where to Watch Birds, J. Gooders (A. Deutsch).

The Book of Bird Watching, R.M. Lockley (A. Barker).

BIRD BEHAVIOUR

Down the Long Wind, G. Christian (Newnes).

The Migration of Birds, J. Fisher (Bodley Head).

Bird Behaviour, D. Goodwin (Museum Press).

Mysteries of Animal Behaviour, T. Jennings (Wheaton/Pergamon).

Animal Navigation, R.M. Lockley (A. Barker).

Bird Migration, R. Spencer (Museum Press).

SOME BOOKS ON INDIVIDUAL SPECIES

The Wren, E.A. Armstrong (Collins).

Birds of Prey, P. Brown (A. Deutsch).

The Redstart, J. Buxton (Collins).

Black-headed Gull, H. Dobinson (Longmans).

Blue Tit, H. Dobinson (Longmans).

Chaffinch, H. Dobinson (Longmans).

Collared Dove, H. Dobinson (Longmans).

House Sparrow, H. Dobinson (Longmans).

Song Thrush, H. Dobinson (Longmans).

The Swallow, E. Hosking and C. Newberry (Collins).

The Life of The Robin, D. Lack (Witherby).

Swifts in a Tower, D. Lack (Methuen).

The Heron, F.A. Lowe (Collins).

The Hawfinch, G. Mountfort (Collins).

The Woodpigeon, R.K. Murton (Collins).

The Yellow Wagtail, S. Smith (Collins).

A Study of Blackbirds, D.W. Snow (Allen and Unwin).

The Lapwing in Britain, K.G. Spencer (Brown).

The House Sparrow, D. Summers-Smith (Collins).

The Herring Gull's World, N. Tinbergen (Collins).

The Life of the Rook, G.K. Yeates (P. Allan).

GENERAL NATURAL HISTORY

The Oxford Book of Insects, J. Burton (Oxford).

The Observer's Book of Pond Life, J. Clegg (Warne).

Shell Nature Lover's Atlas, J. Fisher (Ebury Press).

The Observer's Book of Garden Flowers, A. King (Warne).

Mammals of Britain, their Tracks, Trails and Signs, M.J. Lawrence and R.W. Brown (Blandford).

The Observer's Book of Weather, R.M. Lester (Warne).

Tracks and Signs of British Animals, A. Leutscher (Cleaver Hume).

The Observer's Book of Common Insects and Spiders, E.F. Linssen and L.H. Newman (Warne).

The Pocket Guide to Wild Flowers, D. McClintock and R.S.R. Fitter (Collins).

The Observer's Book of Grasses, Sedges and Rushes, F. Rose (Warne).

Tracks, Trails and Signs, F. Speakman (Bell).

The Observer's Book of Trees, W.J. Stokoe (Warne).

The Observer's Book of Wild Animals of the British Isles, W.J. Stokoe (Warne).

The Observer's Book of Wild Flowers, W.J. Stokoe (Warne).

The Book of Flowering Trees and Shrubs, S.B. Whitehead (Warne).

Some Useful Addresses

The Royal Society for the Protection of Birds is the largest ornithological society, and deals with all aspects of the conservation and protection of birds. It maintains a growing number of bird sanctuaries and has saved some of our rarer birds from extinction. Its publications include the bi-monthly magazine **Birds**, which is free to members, and a number of interesting guides and leaflets on birds. Address: The Lodge, Sandy, Bedfordshire.

The Young Ornithologists' Club is a junior branch of the R.S.P.B. It publishes a quarterly magazine **Bird Life** and runs day and holiday courses on bird watching in many parts of Great Britain, and has a network of adult bird-watchers throughout the country ready to take out beginners in their own area. Address: The Lodge, Sandy, Bedfordshire.

The British Trust for Ornithology is essentially concerned with bird research. The Trust runs the national bird-ringing scheme and organizes surveys and censuses on a national scale. It publishes several guides to field work and a quarterly journal **Bird Study**. Address: Beech Grove, Tring, Hertfordshire.

The Wildfowl Trust is a world organization for the study and conservation of ducks, geese and swans. At Slimbridge and its other wildfowl reserves it has a unique collection of wildfowl including many wild, free-flying birds. Members receive regular Bulletins and an annual publication **Wildfowl**. Address: Slimbridge, Gloucestershire GL2 7BT.

The Wildfowl Trust has a junior branch called the **Goslings**.

The British Naturalists' Association covers all aspects of natural history and nature conservation, including birds, for adults and young people. Its magazine **Country-Side** is published three times a year. Address: Willowfield, Boyneswood Road, Four Marks, Alton, Hampshire.

Every county has a **County Naturalists' Trust** whose main function is the creation of bird sanctuaries and nature reserves. In addition, most towns of any size have an ornithological society, or a natural history society with a bird-watching section. The address of your local naturalists' trust, ornithological society or natural history society can be obtained by writing to the **Council for Nature**, c/o Zoological Society of London, Regent's Park, London NW1 4RY, enclosing a stamped addressed envelope.

The Wildlife Youth Service encourages young people to take a much greater and more active interest in the study and preservation of the world's wildlife and wild places. It organizes adventure camp holidays, arranges field study rambles, lectures, meetings and film programmes. It provides a free information service to deal with members' questions on wildlife and conservation matters and maintains contact with its members by Newsletter and the official WYS magazine—**Animals**. Address: Wallington, Surrey.